GLAMOROUS COCKTAILS

GLAMOROUS COCKTAILS

FASHIONABLE MIXES FROM ICONIC LONDON BARS

WILLIAM YEOWARD

CICO BOOKS

LONDON NEW YORK

For Miss Poppy
who never touched a drop!

Published in 2018 by CICO Books
An imprint of Ryland Peters & Small Ltd
341 E 116th St, New York, NY 10029
20–21 Jockey's Fields, London WC1R 4BW

www.rylandpeters.com

10 9 8 7 6 5

First published in 2012 by CICO Books
as *William Yeoward's American Bar*

Text copyright © William Yeoward 2012
Design and photography copyright
© CICO Books 2012

A CIP catalog record for this book is
available from the Library of Congress
and the British Library.

ISBN: 978 1 78249 646 5

Printed in China

Project editor: Gillian Haslam
Design: Paul Tilby
Photography: Gavin Kingcome
Illustration on endpapers: Roger Hall

ACKNOWLEDGMENTS

Of all my books I think this one, *Glamorous Cocktails*,
is a real example of team effort. The fact that my
name appears on the jacket must be read as an
umbrella for all mentioned here.

And so I thank:

Tim and Dana Jenkins for masterminding the design and
production of this most beautiful crystal and encouraging
me in my quest for perfection.

Paul Bramfitt, Nicholas Carter, Lisa Gibson-Keynes,
Jenny South, Sam Kingcome, Joe Trinanes, Michael
Williamson, Michael Nicholson, Adam Smith, Mark Brook,
Tracey Leonard, Harry Jenkins, Darren Shick, Danny Parnes,
Kevin Haas, Brian Freidman, Erich Salatin, David Hall,
Haley Felchlin-Brinkworth, Sarah Harris, Gary Cooper,
Kate Coleman, Daniel Nigussie.

The world's most patient bartenders: Erik Lorincz, Agostino
Perrone, Adam Jannese, Christopher Moore, Mickael Perron,
Gianluca Mennella, Antonio Cassino, and Alastair Tatton,
the talented mixologist.

Then the great back-up team of Paul Tilby, Gillian Haslam,
Anna Galkina; my communicator Leonie Highton and Roger
Hall for his delicious endpapers.

My friend and photographer Gavin Kingcome who knows
how to make my crystal sparkle, Cindy Richards who
continues to realize my dreams, David Peters who "gets"
our dreams, and Colin, who we hope will sample the
delights herein.

MIX
Paper | Supporting
responsible forestry
FSC® C008047
FSC
www.fsc.org

CONTENTS

INTRODUCTION

NO OTHER DRINKS CAN MATCH COCKTAILS FOR SHEER GLAMOUR. IT'S NOT JUST THE UNIQUE FLAVORS, GORGEOUS COLORS, AND EXQUISITE PRESENTATION THAT I LOVE; IT'S ALSO THE HEADY ASSOCIATIONS WITH THOSE MOST GLAMOROUS OF DECADES, THE TWENTIES AND THIRTIES. THE LEGENDARY BARS WHERE THE BEAU MONDE MET FOR THEIR MANHATTANS AND BLOODY MARYS, THE ICONIC STARS WHO ROMANCED OVER EXOTIC "MIXES" IN HOLLYWOOD MOVIES, THE JAZZ, THE CLOTHES... FOR ME, THESE ARE ALL PART OF THE INTOXICATION.

The first references to cocktails go way back but one of the earliest mixes to make a significant impact must surely have been the dry martini. This seems to have made its debut in the States at the end of the nineteenth century and, to this day, remains a classic—though the definitive recipe is the subject of much dispute among aficionados. The dry martini, along with the many other forms of cocktails that appeared, soon became all the rage, and it didn't take long for the essentially American concept of the cocktail to catch on in Europe. The fashionable bars that sprang up as a result in London and Paris and on the Côte d'Azur in the Twenties and Thirties were often known as "American bars," alluding to the trans-Atlantic origins of the drinks they served.

For me, the term "American bar" never fails to conjure an aura of glamour and romance. However, the early days of cocktails were also touched with decadence and intrigue, and I suspect it was those qualities that especially appealed to me when I was a child and first became curious about these drinks. I can remember thinking how quaint it was when I watched that wonderfully funny film *Some Like it Hot*—which is still my favorite movie today— and saw people drinking "odd" things out of teacups. I didn't understand about the effects of alcohol, and I had no idea what was going on, as I had never been told about Prohibition,

speakeasies, and bootlegging. When all was explained to me, though, it simply struck me as naughtily glamorous, magical even.

The glamour of cocktails comes across more overtly in many earlier movies, such as *Top Hat*, starring the impeccably attired Fred Astaire and Ginger Rogers, and *It Happened One Night*, with Claudette Colbert and Clark Gable, both of which premiered in the mid-Thirties. There, you see the actors raising glasses unmistakably filled with alcoholic concoctions. My own initiation into the world of cocktails came when my father took me to the cocktail bar of a swish hotel before going on to see Marlene Dietrich performing live during one of her tours to Britain. The very thought of being allowed into what I imagined to be a den of quaffing iniquity completely captivated me. I suddenly felt very grown-up.

Since then, I have visited any number of cocktail bars. In fact, you could say that the pursuit of cocktails has led me to many of the

best treats I can think of in life: sky bars at the top of Asian hotels, where the heat and humidity outside are countered indoors by mojitos in ice-cold glasses; sophisticated venues in Venice and Rome, where international chic reigns supreme; Far Eastern "oases," where musk and cardamom scent the air and many different lives converge; Hollywood, where every barista is an Adonis, and girls who never age sit in perfect, snakelike form on heavily chromed and leathered stools; and tropical islands, where beach-babes splash as they sip in shallow pools shaded by palms. These always provide moments of idyllic pleasure.

in when you are socializing in a group as when you are having a quiet drink *à deux*. And it should always allow you to see the bartender doing his stuff. All that slick mixing, shaking, pouring, and garnishing... what a waste if you can't watch a true artist at work and marvel at the speed and confidence!

As for the cocktails themselves, there are literally thousands of recipes to choose from, and there are more appearing virtually by the minute, so it would be impossible not to find one to match every sentiment and occasion, whether a celebration marking a highlight in the journey of life, a greeting, a first date, the closure of a deal, a surreptitious flirt, or simply a "stop" at the end of the day. Cocktails can reflect times of affection, of closeness, of private thought, or, most often, feelings of companionship and gaiety.

COCKTAILS CAN REFLECT TIMES OF AFFECTION, OF CLOSENESS, OF PRIVATE THOUGHT, OR, MOST OFTEN, FEELINGS OF COMPANIONSHIP AND GAIETY

Great bars are fusions of good design, perfect service, and, of course, deliciously mixed cocktails. The room needs to be comfortable and have "atmosphere," but it shouldn't be so darkly intimate that you can't find your way to a table, and nor should it be so bland that it kills any sense of fun or friendship. Ideally, a bar should be so well designed that it is as enjoyable to be

and styles, depending on whether the mix is long or short, served "straight up," or on the rocks.

If I'm giving a party at home, rather than just asking round three or four friends, I usually get in some help, as I want to spend as much time as possible chatting to my guests. For those gatherings, I've got together a little team, who are brilliant at making everything run smoothly. There's Alastair, who mixes the cocktails, Kate, who makes the most wonderful canapés, and Daniel, the butler. As you can see from the photographs here, which were taken at a party in my apartment in London, this trio makes my life very easy. (You can find some of Alastair's cocktail recipes and Kate's canapé recipes in the chapter at the end of the book—along with numerous useful tips and terms.)

Although, over the years, I have learnt a lot about cocktails, I don't pretend to be in the same league as the best professionals, such as the internationally acclaimed maestros who work in the five London cocktail bars that I especially love and are featured here. They all have their individual interpretations of the "classics," as well as creating "new" flavors, and they have been generous enough to share some of their secrets with me—and now with you.

BEAUTIFUL CRYSTAL IS THE ULTIMATE ENHANCEMENT FOR ANY DRINK BUT COCKTAILS IN PARTICULAR AFFORD THE OPPORTUNITY TO USE MANY DIFFERENT SHAPES AND STYLES

I make cocktails at home regularly and get enormous enjoyment from preparing—and, in moderation of course, drinking!—them. I love the ritual of balancing the flavors, muddling and stirring, hearing the clink of ice, selecting the right glass, and giving a final flourish with a classic twist of citrus or something more exotic. As someone who is passionate about crystal, I regard the glass as an essential ingredient in achieving the perfect cocktail. Beautiful crystal is the ultimate enhancement for any drink but cocktails in particular afford the opportunity to use many different shapes

THE CONNAUGHT BAR

The Connaught is one of the great hotels of the world, and for me The Connaught Bar,
designed by my talented friend David Collins, is the epitome of Mayfair glamour. In fact,
it won World's Best Cocktail Bar in 2016. I love the appearance and atmosphere, which are
relaxed and comfortable but also stimulating, with lots of chat and exchanges going on.
I enjoy places like this, where the people "dress" and obviously relish the finer things in life.
There's a stunning use of mirror and silver, both of which were typical in the fashionable
bars of the Twenties and Thirties, an era when interior design had an éclat that really strikes
a chord with me. When I was working on this book, the time I spent with the Connaught's
head mixologist, Agostino Perrone, was a highlight. It's always exciting to work with people
who are at the top of their particular tree, and it was clear to me that Agostino is not only
an expert in mixing exquisitely balanced cocktails but also has a lot of fun when he is
performing on his "stage." As in all the best places, there are many little individual touches
that make one's visit even more memorable. For instance, if you glance behind the bar here,
you will see small bottles of the Connaught's homemade bitters, with flavors that have been
perfected after years of experimenting and make all the difference to the cocktails. An
evening at The Connaught Bar sees my humor improve and my shoulders relax!

CONNAUGHT MARTINI

THE GREAT THING ABOUT ORDERING A MARTINI AT THE CONNAUGHT IS THAT YOU CAN HAVE IT PERSONALIZED WITH ONE OF THE BAR'S HOMEMADE BITTERS. THEY COME IN A WHOLE VARIETY OF FLAVORS, WHICH ADD INDIVIDUAL TOUCHES WITHOUT CHANGING THE ESSENTIAL CHARACTER OF THIS CLASSIC COCKTAIL. I'VE TRIED SEVERAL OF THEM AND HAVEN'T YET DECIDED WHICH I LIKE BEST. NEVER MIND, THAT'S A GOOD EXCUSE TO GO BACK AND CARRY ON EXPERIMENTING!

3 drops bitters (such flavors as vanilla, grapefruit, cardamom, licorice, lavender, ginger, coriander)
½oz. (15ml) dry vermouth
3oz. (75ml) vodka (or gin)
To garnish: mist of lemon peel; zest and a twist of lemon peel

Put the bitters into a martini glass and gently swirl. Stir the vermouth and vodka (or gin) over big chunks of ice in a mixing jug. Strain into the martini glass. To finish, hold a piece of lemon peel above the glass and twist/squeeze so that a fine, aromatic mist falls onto the top of the cocktail, then garnish with a lemon twist. (You could substitute Italian, green olives.)

BLOODY MARY

AGOSTINO TELLS ME THAT THIS RECIPE WAS CREATED IN COLLABORATION WITH HIS FRIEND ERIK LORINCZ, WHO IS BARTENDER AT THE SAVOY'S AMERICAN BAR. IT'S A REAL SHOWSTOPPER TO WATCH BEING MADE, AS THE MIX IS POURED–FROM A CONSIDERABLE HEIGHT–FROM ONE SHAKER TO ANOTHER TO AERATE IT. THE PALE LAYER YOU SEE ON TOP IS "CELERY AIR," WHICH I GATHER IS MADE BY JUICING SOME CELERY WITH A LITTLE CELERY SALT AND A SMALL AMOUNT OF THE EMULSIFIER, LECITE.

2oz. (50ml) vodka
3½oz. (100ml) tomato juice
A few dashes Tabasco
Salt and pepper
A little fresh horseradish, grated
A few leaves fresh cilantro (coriander), torn
A few dashes Worcestershire sauce
2 bar spoons (10ml) fresh lemon juice
To garnish: "celery air" (see page 156); grated nutmeg

Stir all the ingredients over ice in a shaker. Strain the mixture into another shaker (without ice); then pour back into the first shaker. Strain into a large short-stemmed coupe glass, without ice, and garnish with the "celery air" and a quick sprinkling of grated nutmeg.

THIS RECIPE IS A VARIATION ON THE OLD-FASHIONED, THE DRINK FAVORED BY DON DRAPER IN "MAD MEN." IT USES JAPANESE WHISKY BUT IT COULD BE MADE WITH MOST OTHER AGED SPIRITS, SUCH AS SCOTCH WHISKY, COGNAC, RUM, TEQUILA, OR, OF COURSE, AMERICAN BOURBON. IT'S SIMPLE, SOPHISTICATED-AND STRONG! IF YOU'RE SERVING A POWERFUL DRINK LIKE THIS, YOU COULD FOLLOW THE CONNAUGHT'S EXAMPLE AND PROVIDE ALONGSIDE IT A JUG OF WATER FLAVORED WITH ORANGE, CUCUMBER, AND MINT. PERSONALLY, I WOULD RECOMMEND DRINKING THE COCKTAIL AND THE FLAVORED WATER IN EQUAL PARTS.

THE SHOGUN OLD-FASHIONED

Stir the ingredients over large chunks of ice in a mixing jug until you achieve the right balance of flavor and temperature. This will depend on the rate of dilution of the ice. Strain into a glass with plenty of ice, squeeze over a mist of orange zest and garnish with the twist of peel.

2oz. (50ml) Japanese single malt whisky (Nikka Yoichi 1988)

2 bar spoons (10ml) homemade sugar syrup

2 dashes Vintage Abbott's Bitters (or Bob's Abbott's Bitters)

To garnish: mist of orange zest; twist of orange peel

MULATA DAISY

BACARDI RUM APPEARS TO HAVE COME INTO FAVOR IN THE TWENTIES, WHEN AMERICANS TRAVELED TO CUBA TO ESCAPE PROHIBITION IN THE STATES. IT'S THE BASIS FOR THIS COCKTAIL, WHICH HAS A SUMPTUOUS, CHOCOLATEY "COLLAR" AROUND THE RIM OF THE GLASS, GIVING AN ELEGANCE THAT RECALLS THE TWENTIES AND REFLECTS THE EXOTIC, ISLAND LOCATION. AGOSTINO, WHO WON AN AWARD FOR HIS MULATA DAISY, TOLD ME IT'S IMPORTANT TO SHAKE THE MIX VIGOROUSLY–TO MAKE IT COME MORE "ALIVE." NOW, WE DO LOVE A LIVELY COCKTAIL!

¾oz. (20ml) fresh lime juice
Cocoa powder
2 bar spoons (10ml) Galliano liqueur
1 bar spoon superfine (caster) sugar
½ bar spoon fennel seeds
1½oz. (40ml) Barcardi rum
¾oz. (20ml) chocolate liqueur

Before juicing the lime, halve it and run a cut surface round the rim of the glass, then carefully dip the rim into cocoa powder to create a soft, chocolatey "collar." Swirl the inside of the glass with the Galliano liqueur, which will give a final bouquet of aniseed and other fresh aromas. Stir the sugar and lime juice together in a shaker; add the fennel seeds and muddle them gently with a stirrer. Add ice, the rum, and chocolate liqueur. Shake vigorously. Double-strain into a coupe glass.

COCKTAILS CAN BRING TO MIND TRAVEL AND DISTANT LANDS.
HERE, THE BARTENDER GIVES A SPIN TO AN ICONIC ITALIAN
COCKTAIL BY SUBTLY EVOKING THE FAR EAST WITH A HINT OF
CARDAMOM. NOTE THAT HE GENTLY SWIRLS, RATHER THAN
SHAKES, THE MIX, AS HE WANTS TO RETAIN THE BUBBLES IN
THE PROSECCO. IT'S A DRINK I LOVE, AND I ALWAYS LOOK
FORWARD TO EATING THE FRESH PEACH GARNISH–AND ANYONE
ELSE'S PEACH, COME TO THAT.

PEACH AND CARDAMOM BELLINI

1 cardamom pod
½oz. (15ml) peach purée
5oz. (150ml) prosecco
To garnish: thin slices
of peach

Break open the cardamom pod and extract the seeds. Gently
muddle the seeds with the peach purée in a mixing jug. Add
ice and the prosecco. Gently swirl, then strain into an very cold
Champagne flute and garnish with the peach slices.

TEA RINFRESCO

ALTHOUGH THE INSPIRATION FOR THIS ALCOHOL-FREE COCKTAIL IS ASIAN, I WAS
INTRIGUED TO LEARN FROM AGOSTINO–WHO, AS WE KNOW, COMES FROM ITALY–THAT
THE "RINFRESCO" IN THE TITLE IS ITALIAN FOR "I REFRESH YOU." AND I CAN PERSONALLY
VOUCH FOR THE FACT THAT TEA RINFRESCO IS INDEED REFRESHING. IT'S THE PERFECT
DRINK FOR A HOT DAY, WHEN YOU WANT SOMETHING LONG AND DELICIOUSLY COOLING.
THINK ELEGANCE BY AN ITALIAN LAKE.

1oz. (30ml) lychee purée
1oz. (30ml) mandarin purée
2 slices fresh ginger, peeled
3½oz. (100ml) organic Earl Grey tea (at room temperature)
¾oz. (20ml) homemade sugar syrup
Soda water, for topping up
To garnish: a Chinese gooseberry; sugar-frosted fresh mint leaves

Shake the ingredients, except the soda water, over ice and double-strain into a highball glass with ice. Garnish with the Chinese gooseberry and mint leaves. Top up with the soda water.

THE MANHATTAN HAS BEEN AROUND FOR A LONG TIME AND IS PROBABLY THE NEAREST RIVAL TO THE MARTINI IN THE COCKTAIL STAKES. THE RECIPE BELOW IS A VARIATION ON THE THEME AND ILLUSTRATES ONE OF THE THINGS THAT FASCINATE ME MOST ABOUT MIXED DRINKS: THE WAY THE DIFFERENT INGREDIENTS PLAY OFF EACH OTHER. IN THIS MIX, AS THE BARTENDER CONTENDS, THE COFFEE-FLAVORED GALLIANO ENHANCES THE RYE WHISKEY AND GIVES "LENGTH," WHILE THE BLACKBERRY LIQUEUR ADDS A ROUND SWEETNESS AND A PLEASANT SENSATION IN THE MOUTH.

RISTRETTO MANHATTAN

2oz. (50ml) rye whiskey
¾oz. (20ml) sweet vermouth
2 dashes Vintage Abbott's bitters (or Bob's Abbott's Bitters)
2 bar spoons (10ml) Galliano Ristretto (coffee-flavored)
1 bar spoon (5ml) blackberry liqueur
To garnish: mist of orange zest; twist of orange

Stir all the ingredients with ice in a mixing jug and strain into a small wine glass (with or without ice, depending on preference). Mist the orange zest over the cocktail and garnish with a twist of peel.

FLEURISSIMO

1 cube white sugar
5 dashes Peychaud's bitters
1 bar spoon (5ml) violet liqueur
½oz. (15ml) Cognac XO
5oz. (150ml) Champagne, to top up
To garnish: mist of orange zest; a rose petal; a blueberry

I HAD NEVER COME ACROSS A COCKTAIL CALLED FLEURISSIMO BEFORE, BUT I CAN QUITE SEE HOW THIS CHAMPAGNE-BASED CREATION GOT ITS NAME. DIVERGING FROM A TYPICAL CHAMPAGNE COCKTAIL RECIPE, IT HAS LOVELY FLORAL NOTES, THANKS TO THE ADDITION OF THE VIOLET LIQUEUR AND, OF COURSE, THE BEAUTIFUL, BUT SIMPLE, GARNISH OF A ROSE PETAL AND BLUEBERRY. AS A VERY VISUAL PERSON, I CONSIDER IT PARTICULARLY APPEALING BECAUSE IT LOOKS AS GOOD AS IT TASTES.

Hold the sugar cube in tongs and drip the bitters onto it. Gently drop the cube into a Champagne flute. Pour in the violet liqueur and Cognac, then top up with the Champagne. Mist with the orange zest and decorate with a rose petal and a blueberry.

OF ALL THE COCKTAILS THAT AGOSTINO HAS DEVISED, THIS MUST BE THE CLOSEST TO HIS HEART, BECAUSE THE INGREDIENTS PAY HOMAGE TO THREE PLACES IMPORTANT IN HIS LIFE: GIN FROM LONDON, SHERRY FROM SPAIN, AND LIMONCELLO FROM HIS HOME COUNTRY, ITALY. THE COLORS ALSO REPRESENT THE ITALIAN TRICOLORE FLAG. AGOSTINO RECOMMENDS GIN FROM SIPSMITH'S DISTILLERY, WHERE HIS FRIEND, SPIRIT HISTORIAN JARED BROWN, IS MASTER DISTILLER.

TRICOLORE

Shake all the ingredients over ice and double-strain into a pre-chilled glass. (If you have used ice to chill the glass, discard it.) Garnish with the cherry and lime twist.

1½oz. (40ml) London dry gin

2 bar spoons (10ml) Limoncello di Amalfi

½oz. (15ml) fino sherry

2 bar spoons (10ml) homemade vanilla-infused sugar syrup (see page 157)

¾oz. (20ml) fresh lemon juice

To garnish: a marinated cherry and lime twist

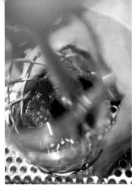

A WONDERFUL ASPECT OF WORKING WITH THE BARTENDERS ON THIS BOOK WAS THAT WE WOULD OFTEN GO OFF-PISTE. WHEN I TOLD THEM THE SORT OF FLAVORS I LIKE, THEY WOULD COME UP WITH A NEW COCKTAIL ON THE SPUR OF THE MOMENT. NOW THAT'S WHAT I CALL PROFESSIONALISM! AGOSTINO MIXED THIS VARIATION ON A COBBLER SPECIALLY FOR ME DURING OUR PHOTOGRAPHY SESSION. CARLOS PLACE REFERS TO THE CONNAUGHT'S ADDRESS.

CARLOS PLACE COBBLER

4 or 5 fresh raspberries
1½oz. (40ml) Zubrowka bison grass vodka
½oz. (15ml) tawny port
2 bar spoons (10ml) fresh lemon juice
4 or 5 drops chocolate liqueur
½oz. (15ml) homemade
vanilla sugar
2 bar spoons (10ml) Galliano Balsamico
(balsamic flavored)
To garnish: grated dark chocolate and
grated tonka bean

Muddle the raspberries in a mixing jug, then add the rest of the ingredients. Stir with ice and strain into a goblet or wine glass with ice. Garnish with the grated chocolate and tonka bean.

"THIS IS A DRINK WITH BALLS—ICE BALLS!" SO SAID AGOSTINO, WHICH MADE ME SHRIEK WITH LAUGHTER WHEN I HEARD IT. I NOTICED HE MADE THE BALLS IN A FIENDISH, METAL DEVICE, WHICH HE APPEARED TO FILL WITH ICE AND THEN, AS IF BY MAGIC, OUT POPPED A PERFECT CRYSTAL SPHERE. AS FOR THE COCKTAIL ITSELF, THE ENERGIZING QUALITIES OF THE GINSENG ARE HAPPILY BALANCED BY THE MELLOWNESS OF THE BENECTINE. DELICIOUS!

YELLOW SUBMARINE

1½oz. (40ml) Calle 23 tequila
¾oz. (20ml) Kammerling's Ginseng Spirit
2 bar spoons (10ml) Benedictine
To garnish: pineapple "leaf"; pineapple slices topped with cinnamon sugar, caramelized with a cook's blowtorch

Stir all the ingredients with ice in a mixing jug, then strain into a glass with a large ball of ice. Garnish with a pineapple "leaf" and some caramelized slices of pineapple on the side.

NEGRONI

1oz. (25ml) Martini Rosso vermouth
1oz. (25ml) gin
1oz. (25ml) Campari
To garnish: orange wedges

THIS IS SURELY THE ITALIAN COCKTAIL PAR EXCELLENCE. ITS FLAVOR IS A SPLENDID FUSION OF SWEETNESS, SPICINESS, AND BITTERNESS, GIVING IT A PARTICULAR KIND OF "STRENGTH" THAT AGOSTINO CONSIDERS TO BE A REFLECTION OF THE ITALIAN CHARACTER. AN ADDED REASON WHY I ENJOY IT SO MUCH MAY BE TO DO WITH ITS APPEARANCE. AS SOMEONE WITH A PASSION FOR COLOR, I FIND IT REALLY HITS THE SPOT IN THAT DEPARTMENT. OR PERHAPS, SECRETLY, I'M JUST A LITTLE BIT ITALIAN!

Fill an old fashioned glass with ice. (Ideally, use "hard" ice—see page 157.) Pour in the ingredients and gently stir. Garnish with the orange wedges.

I'VE ALWAYS THOUGHT THAT DIFFERENT COLORED LADIES IN COCKTAIL BARS WERE RATHER JOLLY–INCLUDING GREEN ONES. THE ASIAN SLANT IN THIS RECIPE COMES FROM THE JUICE OF THE YUZU, A CITRUS FRUIT GROWN IN JAPAN, WHICH HAS A DISTINCTIVE FLAVOR DESCRIBED BY SOME PEOPLE AS A CROSS BETWEEN MANDARIN AND GRAPEFRUIT, THOUGH OTHERS THINK IT'S MORE LIKE A SYNTHESIS OF LIME AND GRAPEFRUIT. A SUBTLE DIFFERENCE! SEE WHAT YOU THINK WHEN YOU TRY IT.

1 egg white
1½oz. (40ml) Calvados
½oz. (15ml) yuzu juice
¾oz. (20ml) homemade sugar syrup infused with cucumber peel (see page 157)
1 bar spoon (5ml) absinthe
1 bar spoon matcha green-tea powder
Dash fresh apple juice
To garnish: a mist of lavender bitters; apple slice with a drop of bitters on it

GREEN LADY

Put the egg white in a shaker and stir to break it down. (The egg white gives a lovely, rounded, silky texture to the cocktail.) Add the rest of the ingredients and ice. Shake, then strain into a glass. Garnish with a mist of lavender bitters, sprayed from an atomizer, and the slice of apple.

THIS COCKTAIL IS LACED WITH THE BRAZILIAN SPIRIT, CACHAÇA, WHICH IS MADE FROM FERMENTED SUGAR CANE AND REMINDS ME SOMEWHAT OF RUM. THE CINNAMON SUGAR ENHANCES THE SOUTH AMERICAN AURA OF THE COCKTAIL–AS DOES THE PUMPKIN GOURD OF COCONUT WATER THAT THE CONNAUGHT SERVES WITH IT, TO PROVIDE "REFRESHMENT" AND GIVE THE BRAZILIAN DRUM LENGTH. THE WHOLE ENSEMBLE IS ONE OF THOSE GRASS-SKIRT, DESERT-ISLAND MOMENTS, WHICH IS ODD– BUT FUN–TO EXPERIENCE IN LONDON.

BRAZILIAN DRUM

½ lime, cut in pieces
2 bar spoons cinnamon sugar
2oz. (50ml) cachaça

Muddle the lime and cinnamon sugar in an exotic serving vessel. Add crushed ice and the cachaça; stir with a swizzle stick.

ANNABEL'S

There's nothing like a good dance to generate a feeling of relaxation and enjoyment, and I can think of no better place for this than Annabel's club in London's Berkeley Square, which opened in 1963 and moved to a beautiful Grade I listed Georgian mansion house on the same square in 2018. I am drawn to the dark, cozy interior, with its comfortable upholstery and candlelight, and to the music, which I judge to be brilliantly cross-generational. Altogether, Annabel's provides a memorable setting, as effective for a dinner for two as for a private party encompassing the whole club. My idea of a wonderful evening here includes a meal of fresh crab, followed by some tasty game—my favorite being venison—washed down with gorgeous vintages from the club's renowned cellar. However, before I settle down to the food, I am invariably to be found by the bar, where Mickael Perron and Gianluca Mennella are ready to mix their splendid confections. I like to vary my choices but if I have a moment's hesitation, I frequently revert to asking Mickael for one of the club's delectable Alfresco Bellinis or Gianluca for the famous Annabel's Special.

SMOKED OLD-FASHIONED

1 brown sugar cube
6 drops Angostura bitters
1oz. (25ml) Laphroaig 15-year-old single malt whisky
2oz. (50ml) Maker's Mark bourbon whiskey
To garnish: a large orange twist and a black cherry

THE MEREST SNIFF OF A SINGLE MALT WHISKY TAKES ME STRAIGHT TO THE HIGHLANDS OF SCOTLAND. TO ME, A SINGLE MALT EVOKES PEAT, HEATHER, CRYSTAL-CLEAR STREAMS, AND PUREST FRESH AIR. TO FIND A COCKTAIL THAT EMPLOYS BOTH 15-YEAR-OLD LAPHROAIG SINGLE MALT AND MAKER'S MARK BOURBON CAN ONLY BE A ROARING SUCCESS. THIS SMOKY VERSION OF THE CLASSIC OLD-FASHIONED IS A ROBUST DRINK AND INTENDED TO BE DRUNK SLOWLY. AS THE ICE MELTS, THE FLAVOR DEVELOPS.

Place the sugar cube on a napkin and drip the Angostura onto the cube. (It is all too easy to drip too much bitters onto the sugar if you put the cube straight into the glass. A napkin will absorb any excess.) Transfer the soaked cube to an old fashioned glass and add the rest of the ingredients. Using the back of a bar spoon, crush the sugar cube to dissolve it into the whiskies. Add large cubes of ice and stir. Garnish with the orange twist and cherry.

AS A GLOBAL TRAVELER, I'VE COME TO REALIZE THAT JUST ABOUT EVERY
BAR IN THE WORLD CLAIMS TO SERVE "CLASSIC" MARTINIS AND YET, IN
MANY CASES, THESE DRINKS DIFFER CONSIDERABLY FROM ONE TO ANOTHER.
I'VE DRUNK THESE SO-CALLED "CLASSICS" IN PLACES AS FAR APART AS
BANGKOK AND SYDNEY, RIO AND LA, BUT FORTUNATELY I DON'T HAVE TO
TRAVEL TO THE ENDS OF THE EARTH TO ENJOY ANNABEL'S EXCELLENT
RENDERING OF THIS COCKTAIL.

ANNABEL'S CLASSIC MARTINI

½oz. (15ml) dry vermouth
3oz. (75ml) Stolichnaya
vodka
Twist of lemon rind
To garnish: 2 unstuffed,
green olives

Pour the vermouth and vodka over ice in a
mixing jug. Stir to make the cocktail very cold.
Strain into a martini glass. Hold the lemon peel
over the glass and twist to spray a fine mist of
its oils onto the cocktail. Discard the rind and
garnish the martini with the olives speared on
a cocktail pick.

RASPERRY AND ROSE MOJITO

BEING A MOJITO-LOVER, I WAS MORE THAN PLEASED TO SEE THAT ONE OF ANNABEL'S SIGNATURE COCKTAILS IS A RASPBERRY AND ROSE MOJITO. NOT ONLY AM I VERY PARTIAL TO COCKTAILS WITH CRUSHED ICE, BUT THE COLOR OF THIS RASPBERRY-AND-ROSE ENCHANTMENT REALLY LIFTS MY SPIRIT. FURTHERMORE, ROSE SYRUP ALWAYS REMINDS ME OF HAPPY VISITS TO MOROCCO, WHERE I BUY LARGE QUANTITIES OF IT AND OF ROSEWATER TO ENHANCE MY WORLD-FAMOUS—THOUGH I SAY IT MYSELF!—ADAPTATION OF THAT SUMPTUOUS DESSERT, ETON MESS.

½oz. (15ml) rose syrup
8 mint leaves
2oz. (50ml) light rum
Freshly squeezed juice of 1 lime
½oz. (15ml) crème de framboise
(raspberry liqueur)
To garnish: 2 rose petals and a mint sprig

Pour the rose syrup into a highball glass. Add the mint leaves and rum. Delicately press the mint with the back of a bar spoon—you want to extract the flavor without breaking up the leaves. Add the lime juice and enough ice to come two-thirds of the way up the glass. Gently churn with the spoon. Pile up with more crushed ice and drizzle over the crème de framboise. Garnish with the rose petals and mint.

SOME 15 OR MORE YEARS AGO, WHEN I FIRST HAD THIS COCKTAIL, I UNDERSTOOD WHY EVERYTHING I'D HEARD ABOUT ANNABEL'S LEGENDARY BARTENDER AT THE TIME, SIDNEY, WAS NOT ONLY TRUE BUT UNDERSTATED. SADLY, I NEVER HAD THE CHANCE TO CONGRATULATE HIM PERSONALLY ON HIS INVENTION OF ANNABEL'S SPECIAL, BUT THERE'S NO QUESTION IN MY MIND THAT THE CLUB'S CURRENT BARTENDERS, WHO REGARD THIS DRINK AS A TRIBUTE TO SIDNEY, ARE ADEPT AT RECREATING IT.

ANNABEL'S SPECIAL

¾oz. (20ml) Benedictine
¾oz. (20ml) Cointreau
¾oz. (20ml) fresh lime juice
1oz. (25ml) Martini Bianco dry vermouth

Pour all the ingredients into a cocktail shaker. Fill with ice and shake. Strain into a coupe glass.

1 lemon
Sea salt and freshly ground black pepper
5oz. (150ml) best-quality tomato juice
½oz. (15ml) lemon juice
½oz. (15ml) Worcestershire sauce
Tabasco, to taste
1¼oz. (35ml) vodka
3 sprinkles celery salt, preferably homemade
To garnish: ½ cherry tomato and a tiny basil leaf

I'VE OFTEN WONDERED WHO MARY, OF BLOODY MARY FAME, WAS, BUT EVEN SEARCHING THROUGH AUTHORITATIVE TOMES HASN'T REVEALED A DEFINITIVE ANSWER. I'M CURIOUS, TOO, AS TO WHY THIS COCKTAIL IS SOMETIMES DESCRIBED AS A HANGOVER CURE. TO ME, THAT EQUATES IT TO SOMETHING IN THE MEDICINE CHEST, TO BE BROUGHT OUT ONLY AFTER A TOO-GOOD DINNER THE NIGHT BEFORE, WHEREAS I THINK IT'S THE PERFECT LUNCHTIME COCKTAIL, HOWEVER YOU FEEL. DON'T DRINK THIS VERSION THROUGH A STRAW OR YOU'LL MISS OUT ON THE SALT-AND-PEPPER RIM.

BLOODY MARY

First, prepare the glass with a salt-and-pepper rim: cut a lemon in half and run the cut surface round the rim, then dip the rim into a mixture of 1 part sea-salt flakes and 1 part freshly ground black pepper. For the cocktail, put all the ingredients into a shaker and slowly "roll" to mix and chill the contents—do not shake aggressively. Strain into the prepared glass and garnish with the tomato and basil leaf on a cocktail pick.

ALMOND ESPRESSO MARTINI

WHEN I WAS SITTING IN A CAFÉ IN ST MARK'S SQUARE IN VENICE AND SPIED AN AFFOGATO BEING MADE–VANILLA ICE CREAM WITH A SHOT OF ESPRESSO POURED OVER IT–I WONDERED IF IT WAS THIS INDULGENT CONFECTION THAT LOOSELY INSPIRED ALMOND ESPRESSO MARTINI. I SAY "LOOSELY" BECAUSE THE COCKTAIL IS RATHER LESS INNOCENT, BEING COMPOSED OF AMARETTO AND VODKA AS WELL AS A COFFEE LIQUEUR. THE AMOUNT OF SUGAR YOU INCLUDE IN THE ESPRESSO IS UP TO YOU–I DON'T LIKE MINE TOO SWEET.

1oz. (25ml) freshly made espresso, sweetened to taste
1¼oz. (35ml) vodka
¾oz. (20ml) amaretto
½oz. (15ml) Kahlúa Coffee liqueur
To garnish: 3 coffee beans and a pinch of toasted, slivered almonds

Pour all the ingredients into a shaker. Fill with ice and shake. Strain into a martini glass. Wait for the cocktail to "separate"—a foam will rise to the top and the liquid below become clearer. Garnish with the coffee beans and almonds.

AL FRESCO BELLINI

I WAS TAKEN ABACK–VERY PLEASANTLY, I SHOULD ADD–WHEN THIS DRINK WAS FIRST PRODUCED FOR ME. EVERY BELLINI I HAD EVER MET BEFORE WAS THE MOST BEAUTIFUL, SOFT SHADE OF PEACHY PINK WHEN IT LANDED IN FRONT OF ME, YET HERE I WAS PRESENTED WITH A DRINK MADE UP OF THREE DIFFERENT-COLORED TIERS: STRONG RED, YELLOW, AND A CREAMY SHADE OF PEACH. IT LOOKED AMAZING. THEN, THE BARTENDER GAVE IT A QUICK STIR AND THE STRIPES MELDED INTO A GENTLE, MAGICAL HUE.

¾oz. (20ml) peach purée
½oz. (15ml) Apérol liqueur
Champagne, chilled, to top up
To garnish: a Chinese gooseberry and a rose petal

To create the three layers, gently pour into the glass each ingredient in turn over the flatter end of a long, double-ended bar spoon. Pour in the peach purée first, then the Apérol, followed by the Champagne. Garnish with the Chinese gooseberry and rose petal. When the Al Fresco Bellini is ready to serve, and is in front of the drinker, stir.

½oz. (20ml) apple schnapps
1½oz. (40ml) vanilla vodka
1oz. (25ml) fresh apple juice
2 bar spoons (10ml) fresh lime juice
2 bar spoons (10ml) sugar syrup
To garnish: alternated, very thin slices of green- and pink-skinned apple; ½ a vanilla bean (pod)

I'M A KEEN COOK–THOUGH VERY MUCH AN AMATEUR, "HOME" ONE–AND I FIND THAT VANILLA IS A GREAT COMPLEMENT TO APPLE, AND I ALWAYS ADD A FEW DROPS OF VANILLA EXTRACT TO MY APPLE DESSERTS. ANNABEL'S BARTENDERS OBVIOUSLY SHARE MY VIEW AS I NOTE THAT THEY USE VANILLA VODKA IN THE CLUB'S APPLE MARTINI. THE COLOR OF THE COCKTAIL COULD BE CONSIDERED QUITE BLAND–UNTIL, THAT IS, THEY GARNISH IT WITH A "BRIDGE" OF THIN SLICES OF APPLE.

APPLE MARTINI

Put all the ingredients into a cocktail shaker filled with ice. Shake. Strain into a martini glass. Garnish with the apple and vanilla. (If the apple slices are freshly cut, they will "stick" together in a row.)

WHEN YOU ARE DEALING WITH STRONG FLAVORS, SUCH AS
BITTERS, YOU HAVE TO BE CAUTIOUS ABOUT THE AMOUNT
OF DROPS OR DASHES YOU USE IN A COCKTAIL. IT'S ALL A
QUESTION OF BALANCE, AND THE BEST BARTENDERS ALWAYS
GET IT RIGHT. HERE, THE HORSE'S NECK, WHICH HAS BEEN
HIGHLY POPULAR AT ANNABEL'S EVER SINCE THE CLUB'S
OPENING IN 1963, IS A FINELY BALANCED EXAMPLE OF
A CLASSIC COCKTAIL THAT I BELIEVE FIRST APPEARED,
IN THE STATES, OVER A CENTURY AGO.

HORSE'S NECK

2oz. (50ml) VSOP Cognac
10 drops Angostura bitters
Ginger ale, to top up
To garnish: lemon twist

Prepare a tall glass with the
"garnish" of a large lemon twist.
Fill with ice cubes and add the
ingredients; then stir.

GREEN PARK

½oz. (15ml) Cointreau
2 bar spoons (10ml) home-made Earl Grey tea syrup
1oz. (25ml) fresh lemon juice
10 fresh basil leaves
1½oz. (40ml) vodka
2oz. (50ml) apple juice
To garnish: fresh basil sprig

BARTENDERS KHALIF HAMZAH AND MATTEO BOSCOLO OF ANNABEL'S INVENTED THIS COCKTAIL IN A COMPETITION TO CREATE A COCKTAIL CELEBRATING THE THIRTIETH ANNIVERSARY OF THE RENOWNED LONDON RESTAURANT, LE CAPRICE, WHICH IS JUST AROUND THE CORNER FROM GREEN PARK. I WAS INTERESTED TO SAMPLE THIS UNUSUAL COMBINATION OF INGREDIENTS, WHICH INCLUDES EARL GREY TEA SYRUP AND BASIL, AND I FOUND IT MUCH TO MY TASTE AND REFRESHING. IT IS SERVED IN A COUPE AND GARNISHED WITH A SPRIG OF BASIL.

Put all the ingredients into a cocktail shaker filled with ice. Shake. Double-strain into a glass. Garnish with the basil.

BERKELEY BLUE BAR

This is an unbeatable spot to take friends who have been shopping themselves to a standstill in one of the most prestigious store areas in the world and are in need of a restorative glass of something special. I remember with joy being invited as a young boy by my paternal grandmother for lunch at the "old" Berkeley hotel, on the corner of Berkeley Street and Piccadilly, where I was mesmerized by the smart ladies in hats sipping elegant drinks in the bar before entering the dining room. The "new" Berkeley, which moved to its present Knightsbridge location some forty years ago, continues to sum up total luxury and refined hospitality and it now has an added air of slicked-up, flicked-up glamour. The Blue Bar has a great zing about it and is one of those places where I could never even contemplate having anything less than a marvellous time. I get an uplifting sense of anticipation when I am heading there, knowing that bartender Adam Jannese mixes a fine Costa Esmeralda—for which I have a particular weakness—and, if I am entertaining a group of friends, that he will produce for me Willie's Spagliata, served in one of my beautiful punch bowls. I've noticed that the bartenders I admire most for their cocktail-making skills—and Adam certainly numbers among them—also have a natural rapport with their guests, which always makes them feel welcome.

SUN CRUSHED

WHEREAS SOME DRINKS WITH THE WORD "SUN" ATTACHED TO THEM MAKE MY MIND RACE TO THE BEACH, HERE I THINK OF ASCOT, WIMBLEDON, HENLEY, AND GLYNDEBOURNE. IT IS A DRINK THAT EVERYONE SEEMS TO ENJOY, BEING SIMULTANEOUSLY SLIGHTLY TANGY AND SLIGHTLY SWEET, AND THEN THERE IS THE FINAL TOPPING UP WITH CHAMPAGNE. IT ALSO LOOKS VERY APPEALING, HAVING A GLORIOUS COLOR. IT MUST HAVE A LOT OF CRUSHED ICE IN IT, AND, OF COURSE, IT SHOULD BE DRUNK THROUGH A STRAW.

3 orange slices
2 bar spoons brown sugar
10 redcurrants
2 bar spoons (10ml) lemon juice
2oz. (60ml) pomegranate liqueur
Champagne, to top up
To garnish: sprig redcurrants and half-slices of orange

Muddle together the orange, sugar, and redcurrants in a highball glass. Add the lemon juice, pomegranate liqueur, and crushed ice. Stir. Top up with Champagne, add more ice, and garnish with the redcurrants and orange slice.

CARAMEL ROB ROY

JUDGING BY THE NAME OF THIS COCKTAIL, THERE CAN'T BE MUCH DOUBT THAT WE SHALL BE HAVING A "WEE DRAM." THE SINGLE MALT WHISKY USED HERE IS FROM THE BOWMORE DISTILLERY, WHICH WAS FOUNDED ON THE ISLAND OF ISLAY IN 1779. THAT WAS JUST TOO LATE FOR POOR OLD ROB ROY HIMSELF TO HAVE HAD THE CHANCE TO SAMPLE THE DISTILLERY'S SMOKILY PEATY NECTAR, BUT HAPPILY IT ISN'T TOO LATE FOR US. WHAT A TREAT SCOTLAND'S MOST FAMOUS FOLK HERO MISSED! THIS COCKTAIL IS BARTENDER ADAM JANNESE'S PERSONAL FAVORITE.

2 bar spoons (10ml) Antica Formula vermouth
2 bar spoons (10ml) Noilly Prat dry vermouth
2 bar spoons (10ml) caramel syrup
2oz. (50ml) Bowmore 12-year-old malt whisky
6 drops orange bitters
To garnish: orange twist

Pour all the ingredients into a shaker or mixing jug. Add ice and stir vigorously. Double-strain into a coupe glass. Mist with the orange twist. Run the twist round the rim of the glass, then drop it gently into the cocktail.

VERLINDEN

EVEN WHEN BARTENDER ADAM IS AT HOME FOR A FAMILY CHRISTMAS,
HIS MIND IS NEVER QUITE "OFF DUTY" WHEN IT COMES TO INVENTING NEW
COCKTAILS. HE TELLS ME THAT HE AND HIS WIFE CREATED THIS VERLINDEN
ON CHRISTMAS MORNING, AFTER BEING GIVEN A HAMPER CONTAINING A
BOTTLE OF PEAR-AND-VANILLA SYRUP. VERLINDEN IS A VERY FESTIVE DRINK,
AND IT IS SIMPLICITY ITSELF TO MAKE, WHICH IS PERFECT ON A DAY WHEN
THERE ARE A MILLION OTHER THINGS TO DO WITHOUT HAVING TO MIX
COMPLICATED COCKTAILS.

1oz. (25ml) Poire Vanille syrup
Champagne, to top up
To garnish: a canned (or bottled) baby pear

Pour the syrup into a Champagne
flute; top up with chilled
Champagne. Stir briefly and
gently—you can use a straw for this
—and garnish with the baby pear.

I'VE COME TO THE CONCLUSION THAT ONE MUSTN'T HAVE PRECONCEIVED NOTIONS WHEN READING THROUGH LISTS OF COCKTAIL INGREDIENTS. FOR INSTANCE, WHEN I FIRST SAW THE LIST FOR APRICOT AND THYME BRONX, I WONDERED ABOUT THE HERB AND WHETHER IT WOULD MAKE A HAPPY MARRIAGE WITH ALL THOSE OTHER FLAVORS. IN FACT, THE SUBTLY AROMATIC THYME WAS SPOT ON–BUT IT IS IMPORTANT TO USE ONLY YOUNG, TENDER SPRIGS. THE THYME GARNISH HEIGHTENS THE CHARM.

APRICOT AND THYME BRONX

Chill a martini glass beforehand. Muddle the thyme and jam in a shaker. Add the other ingredients and top up with ice. Shake. Double-strain into the pre-chilled glass. Garnish with a thyme sprig.

3 sprigs fresh thyme

2 bar spoons apricot jam

2oz. (50ml) No. 209 gin

½oz. (15ml) Noilly Prat dry vermouth

½oz. (15ml) Antica Formula vermouth

1¼oz. (35ml) fresh orange juice

6 drops orange bitters

To garnish: fresh thyme sprig

DRAGON

DRAGONS MAY BE MYTHICAL CREATURES BUT THERE IS NOTHING MYTHICAL ABOUT THIS DRINK. IT'S VERY "REAL" IN EVERY SENSE, WITH GOOD LOOKS AND GOOD FLAVOR. CURIOUSLY, THE BLUE BAR FINDS THAT EVEN PEOPLE WHO DON'T NORMALLY LIKE TEQUILA ARE CONVERTED BY THIS FRUITY, TEQUILA-BASED COCKTAIL. IT HAS A SWEETISH EDGE, BUT IS ALSO FRESH, THANKS TO THE GRAPE ELEMENT AND THE LIME JUICE. IT IS ONE OF THE "SHORT" DRINKS I PARTICULARLY LIKE IN SUMMER.

10 white grapes
2 bar spoons (10ml) fresh lime juice
½oz. (15ml) elderflower cordial
2oz. (50ml) Maestro Dobel Diamond tequila
To garnish: 3 white grapes

Muddle the grapes in a shaker with the lime juice and elderflower cordial. (The grapes should be thoroughly crushed to extract the juice.) Add the tequila and top up with ice. Shake. Double-strain into a martini glass. Garnish with grapes speared on a cocktail pick.

HERE IS ANOTHER TWIST ON A CLASSIC MANHATTAN. AS YOU CAN GUESS BY THE NAME, ADAM'S VERSION HAS THE MOST GLORIOUS AMBER HUE. THERE IS SOMETHING VERY ROMANTIC ABOUT AMBER. IT MAKES ME THINK OF TALES OF ANCIENT ARABIA AND THE EAST, AND EVEN TO THIS DAY AMBER IS GREATLY PRIZED FOR JEWELRY. WITH THE ADDITION OF VANILLA, WHICH IS ALSO ASSOCIATED WITH THE EAST, THE AMBER MANHATTAN IS A JEWEL OF A DRINK.

AMBER MANHATTAN

1½oz. (40ml) Macallan 10-year-old single malt whisky
1 bar spoon (5ml) Macallan Amber Whisky
2 bar spoons (10ml) Martini dry vermouth
2 bar spoons (10ml) Martini Rosso
½oz. (15ml) Cointreau
2 drops orange bitters
To garnish: orange zest

Combine the ingredients in a shaker and top up with ice. Shake. Double-strain into a martini glass. Mist the orange zest over the cocktail, then gently drop it into the glass.

I NEVER THOUGHT I WOULD FIND ANOTHER
COCKTAIL AS REFRESHING AS A MOJITO, BUT
COSTA ESMERALDA MAKES THE GRADE. THIS
DRINK IS MY FAVORITE BLUE BAR CHOICE. IT
WAFTS ME OFF TO PALM-FRINGED BEACHES,
TURQUOISE-BLUE SEAS, AND TROPICAL
SUNSHINE–UNTIL, THAT IS, I COME BACK DOWN
TO EARTH AND REALIZE THAT I AM IN THE
CENTER OF A BIG CITY. STILL, AT LEAST I AM IN A
SUPREMELY COMFORTABLE–AND INCOMPARABLY
STYLISH–PLACE IN THAT CITY.

COSTA ESMERALDA

2 lemon wedges
¾oz. (20ml) lemon juice
2½ bar spoons superfine (caster) sugar
10 fresh basil leaves
2oz. (50ml) Snow Queen vodka
Champagne, to top up
To garnish: a basil leaf and lemon wedge

Muddle the lemon wedges, lemon juice, sugar,
and basil leaves in a shaker. Add the vodka and
half-fill with crushed ice. Lightly shake and strain
into a highball glass. Top up with Champagne.
Blend gently with a bar spoon and add crushed
ice to form a "crown." Garnish with a basil leaf
and lemon wedge.

I HAVE A GREAT FRIEND, SANDY, WHO ADORES THIS COCKTAIL, PROBABLY BECAUSE SHE IS MAD ABOUT BOTH WHISKEY AND PASSION FRUIT. SHE IS IN SEVENTH HEAVEN WHEN SHE HAS A KENTUCKY IN HER HAND, SO MUCH SO THAT IT'S HARD TO GET HER TO CONCENTRATE ON ANYTHING ELSE. I CAN APPRECIATE WHY, AS THE FRUIT AND MINT NOT ONLY BRING A DELICIOUS FRESHNESS TO THE DRINK, BUT ALSO BALANCE THE WARMTH OF THE JACK DANIEL'S.

5 fresh mint leaves
½oz. (15ml) passion fruit purée
1 passion fruit
1oz. (25ml) fresh apple juice
½oz. (15ml) sugar syrup
2oz. (50ml) Jack Daniels single barrel whiskey
To garnish: ½ passion fruit and a fresh mint sprig

KENTUCKY

Muddle the mint with the passion fruit purée in a shaker. Halve the passion fruit and scoop the pulp into the shaker, add the remaining ingredients, and top up with ice. Shake. Double-strain into a martini glass, then garnish with the passion fruit and mint.

THIS IS A COCKTAIL THAT COMES INTO ITS OWN IN THE FALL AND WINTER, WHEN THE INCLUSION OF NUTS IS ESPECIALLY FITTING. ALTHOUGH THE RECIPE HAS A DOUBLE DOSE OF NUTS–WALNUT SYRUP AS WELL AS WALNUT-INFUSED WHISKEY–THE NUTTINESS IS NOT OVERPOWERING. IT IS JUST ENOUGH TO IMBUE A WARM, SEASONAL NOTE. IT IS THE PERFECT FIRESIDE COCKTAIL, AS THE COLOR ECHOES THE FLICKERING FLAMES.

WALNUT AND MAPLE OLD-FASHIONED

Muddle the orange in an old fashioned glass. Add the rest of the ingredients and fill with ice cubes. Stir slowly for a minute or so to allow the ice to dilute the bourbon slightly and for the flavors to develop. Garnish with the orange twist.

2 half-slices orange
2 bar spoons (10ml) maple syrup
2 bar spoons (10ml) walnut syrup
6 drops orange bitters
2oz. (60ml) walnut-infused Eagle Rare 10-year-old bourbon whiskey (see page 157)
To garnish: orange twist

WILLIE'S SPAGLIATA PUNCH BOWL

1 bottle Kammerling's ginseng spirit

7oz. (200ml) Tanqueray gin

15 drops Angostura bitters

8oz. (250ml) Visciolata del Cardinale (Italian cherry liqueur)

Rinds of 10 oranges and 10 lemons

1 bottle Champagne

SOME PEOPLE HAVE STARS NAMED AFTER THEM, I GET COCKTAILS! THIS ONE WAS SPECIALLY MIXED FOR ME BY BARTENDER ADAM WHO, JUST FOR THE SHEER PLEASURE OF IT, TRANSFERRED THE CHAMPAGNE FROM THE BOTTLE TO A BEAUTIFUL, TALL, SLENDER PITCHER BEFORE POURING IT INTO THE PUNCH BOWL. (THE PITCHER IS DESIGNED TO RETAIN THE CHAMPAGNE BUBBLES FOR AS LONG AS POSSIBLE. IT ISN'T NECESSARY TO DECANT CHAMPAGNE BUT IT DOES MAKE A LUXURIOUS SPECTACLE.) THE BOWL, WHICH, ALONG WITH THE PITCHER, WE HAVE INCLUDED IN OUR COLLECTION, IS DECORATED WITH WISTERIA VINES AND HOLDS ENOUGH TO SERVE 8 PEOPLE.

Put all the ingredients, except the fruit rinds and Champagne, into a punch bowl. Stir with the ladle. Add plenty of ice. Mist with the rinds, then add them to the bowl. Pour in the Champagne. Stir once more, gently, then serve.

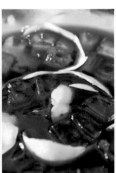

BEAUFORT BAR
AT THE SAVOY

Luxury and comfort are two things I can't resist, so when I visited the Savoy hotel after its extensive renovation, I was greatly relieved to find that these qualities still flourish there in abundance. Walking into a big space can sometimes feel challenging—but not at the Savoy's Beaufort Bar, where one feels embraced by the room rather than intimidated by its large scale. The Art-Deco-inspired design is dark in the best possible way, producing a sense of intimacy, with gold, black, and touches of silver employed to splendid effect. Center-stage is the energetic, talented, and witty bartender, Christopher Moore, who understands that a good conversation is as important as a good cocktail. Surveying his glittering arena, I realize that a great deal of experience must be required for anyone even to begin to think about creating the sort of magical drinks he dispenses. There are so many aspects that, as an amateur, one simply doesn't know about, and it's fun to let a maestro take one on a grand tour of the ingredients—from Yellow Chartreuse and jasmine pearl tea to violet liqueur and Cherry Heering—and to discuss the possibilities they offer for mixing and imaginative presentation. The Savoy hotel has always been a center of excellence, as has the adjoining Savoy Theatre, which I venture to say must be one of the smallest and most charming opera houses in the world when used for Gilbert and Sullivan's delightful productions.

2oz. (50ml) Hendrick's gin
½oz. (15ml) Yellow Chartreuse
1oz. (30ml) freshly squeezed lemon juice
½oz. (15ml) homemade sugar syrup
infused with green tea and cucumber peel
(see page 157)
1 bar spoon lime marmalade
To garnish: 2 dried rose buds (suitable for
using in drinks)

A NUMBER OF THE ROOMS AND COCKTAILS AT THE SAVOY HOTEL CELEBRATE GILBERT AND SULLIVAN'S COMIC VICTORIAN OPERAS, WHICH MADE THEIR DEBUT AT THE SAVOY THEATRE NEXT DOOR. THIS COCKTAIL IS CALLED AFTER PATIENCE, THE HEROINE OF THE OPERA OF THE SAME NAME, WHO WAS A MILKMAID. SHE MIGHT HAVE FOUND THIS TWIST ON A WHITE LADY A BIT STRONGER THAN HER USUAL STOCK-IN-TRADE! THE LIME MARMALADE ADDS TEXTURE AND A LOVELY, TART TASTE.

PATIENCE

Chill a coupe glass. Combine all the ingredients in a cocktail shaker, top up with ice. Shake vigorously. Double-strain into the chilled glass. Garnish with the rose buds.

ELIXIR

KAMMERLING'S GINGSENG SPIRIT IS MADE UP OF OVER 45 DIFFERENT BOTANICALS, WHICH IS PROBABLY WHY CHRISTOPHER SAYS THAT THE CHARACTER OF THIS COCKTAIL HAS AS AN "APOTHECARY" NUANCE–HENCE THE NAME ELIXIR. IT'S FINISHED OFF WITH A MISTING OF JASMINE ESSENCE, NOT JUST ON THE TOP OF THE DRINK BUT ALSO ON THE GLASS. THAT MEANS YOU GET THE SCENT OF JASMINE ON YOUR FINGERS WHILE YOU ARE DRINKING THE COCKTAIL. IT'S A KIND OF MULTI-SENSORY EXPERIENCE.

¾oz. (20ml) Kammerling's Gingseng Spirit
¾oz. (20ml) sugar syrup
1oz. (30ml) jasmine pearl tea (chilled)
5oz. (150ml) Champagne
To garnish: jasmine essence; fresh violets

Combine all the ingredients in a shaker. Top up with ice. Stir very gently and very briefly—this "freshens" and cools the Champagne with the ice, whilst ensuring that it is evenly distributed. Strain into a Champagne flute. Garnish with the violets, and spray the jasmine essence over the drink and the glass (you can use an atomizer for this).

THE IMPRESSIONIST

THE GREAT FRENCH IMPRESSIONIST CLAUDE MONET USED TO STAY AT THE
SAVOY AND HE IS THE INSPIRATION FOR THE COCKTAIL'S TITLE. THE RECIPE
INCLUDES VIOLET AND RASPBERRY FLAVORS, WHICH HAVE A HEAVENLY
AFFINITY, BUT THE REAL TREAT FOR ME IS THE PRESENTATION. THE
IMPRESSIONIST IS SERVED WITH A SIDE GLASS OF DRY ICE AND ROSEWATER,
GARNISHED WITH A ROSE HEAD. THIS ISN'T FOR DRINKING BUT IT CREATES
AN ETHEREAL ROSE MIST AND FRAGRANCE. MY GUESTS ARE ALWAYS AMAZED.

½oz. (15ml) Cherry Marnier
½oz. (15ml) homemade raspberry syrup
1 bar spoon (5ml) Miclo Violette liqueur
Champagne, to top up
To serve: a side glass of dry ice and
rosewater with a rose head or two

Combine the ingredients in a cocktail shaker; fill
up with ice. Shake; then double-strain into a glass.
Top up with Champagne.

AS IN THE COCKTAIL CALLED PATIENCE (SEE PAGE 88), THE NAME OF THIS DRINK REFERS TO A GILBERT AND SULLIVAN OPERA; HERE, IT'S THE SORCERER. THE STORY REVOLVES AROUND SOME VILLAGERS WHO, THANKS TO A POWERFUL APHRODISIAC, ARE ALL IN LOVE. WHETHER THE BEAUFORT'S COCKTAIL HAS THE SAME EFFECT, WHO KNOWS? I DO KNOW, HOWEVER, THAT IT'S A PERSONAL FAVORITE OF THE BARTENDER–WHO USUALLY DRINKS IT AFTER DINNER–AND I CAN CERTAINLY UNDERSTAND WHY. THE SORCERER IS A UNIQUE BALANCING ACT OF FIRST-RATE INGREDIENTS, WHILE THE ORANGE WEDGE PROVIDES A FINAL FLOURISH TO ITS COLOR STORY.

THE SORCERER

1½oz. (40ml) Hennessey Cognac
¾oz. (20ml) Campari
¾oz. (20ml) Gancia Rosso (Italian vermouth)
¾oz. (20ml) Cherry Heering
To garnish: slim orange wedge

Ideally serve this drink over triple-frozen ice (see page 157), which stays much colder than regular cubes. This means that the drink dilutes at a slower rate and remains at the ideal temperature for much longer. Combine all the ingredients in a mixing glass over ice. Stir for about 10 seconds, until the mixture is ice-cold, then strain into a small, chilled carafe. For presentation, pour the cocktail from the carafe into the glass (with ice and orange garnish in it) in front of the drinker.

GIN LANE

TO ME, BOMBAY SAPPHIRE HAS ALWAYS SEEMED A VERY EXOTIC
NAME FOR A GIN. IT MAKES ME THINK OF THE BRITISH RAJ
AND MAGNIFICENT JEWELS. THE PARTICULAR SAPPHIRE
REFERRED TO HERE IS THE 182-CARAT "STAR OF BOMBAY"
AT THE SMITHSONIAN INSTITUTION. IT'S QUITE A ROCK–
AND GIN LANE IS QUITE A COCKTAIL. TO TOP OFF THE TREAT,
THE GARNISH INCLUDES A MARINATED CHERRY, WHICH
CHRISTOPHER HAS PREPARED HIMSELF WITH CHERRY
LIQUEUR, ANGOSTURA BITTERS, AND SUGAR SYRUP.

1 ½oz. (40ml) Bombay Sapphire gin
2 bar spoons (10ml) apricot liqueur
2 bar spoons (10ml) Grand Marnier
1oz. (25ml) freshly squeezed lemon juice
¾oz. (20ml) Orgeat almond syrup
Ginger ale, to top up
To garnish: a sprig of fresh mint and a marinated cherry

Combine the ingredients in a shaker; fill up with
ice. Shake; then strain into a highball glass. Top
up with ginger ale. Fill up with ice cubes and
garnish with the mint and cherry.

CHRISTOPHER TELLS ME HE INVENTED THIS FRESH, CLEAN DRINK AS A SUMMER ALTERNATIVE TO PIMM'S. I CAN'T WAIT TO OFFER IT WHEN I HAVE PARTIES IN MY GARDEN IN THE COUNTRY–IT LOOKS SO BEAUTIFUL, WITH THREE KINDS OF BERRIES TRAPPED BETWEEN LAYERS OF ICE. SERVE THE COCKTAIL IN A WINE GLASS AND LET SIT FOR A FEW MOMENTS TO ALLOW THE FLAVORS OF THE FRUIT TO DEVELOP. ET VOILÀ–YOU GET THE IDEAL CONFECTION FOR A SUNNY GATHERING.

Approximately 5oz. (150ml) Champagne
1 strawberry, cut into 4 pieces
1 blackberry
2 raspberries
2 bar spoons (10ml) elderflower liqueur
¾oz. (20ml) rhubarb liqueur

CELEBRATION CUP

Fill a wine glass two-fifths with Champagne. Add three cubes of ice, then the fruit and the liqueurs. Top up with more ice and more Champagne.

PRINCESS IDA

½oz. (15ml) Grey Goose vodka
¾oz. (20ml) Cherry Heering
1oz. (25ml) fresh lemon juice
¾oz. (20ml) vanilla syrup
1 bar spoon (5ml) pasteurized egg white
3 fresh raspberries
To garnish: 1 fresh raspberry

HERE IS ANOTHER COCKTAIL HONORING ONE OF GILBERT AND SULLIVAN'S MUSICAL MASTERPIECES, "PRINCESS IDA." THE PRINCESS HERSELF DOESN'T SEEM TO HAVE HAD MUCH TIME FOR MEN AND WENT OFF TO RUN A WOMEN'S COLLEGE–WELL, SOME PEOPLE ARE BORN TO WORK! TO ME, THE OPERA AND THE COCKTAIL ARE SO DELICIOUSLY ENTERTAINING THAT THEY COULDN'T FAIL TO APPEAL TO BOTH SEXES. GREY GOOSE VODKA IS THE PERFECT SPIRIT FOR CREATING THIS DRINK.

Combine the ingredients in a shaker; fill up with ice. Shake vigorously; then double-strain into a glass. Garnish with a raspberry.

2oz. (60ml) Oxley gin
1oz. (30ml) Tokaji
1 bar spoon (5ml) sugar syrup
To garnish: lemon peel

NEW DAWN

WITH ITS AMBER GLOW AND "COLD" PRESENCE, THE APPROPRIATELY NAMED NEW DAWN SUBTLY SUGGESTS THE EARLY MORNING. THE FIRST TIME I HAD THIS COCKTAIL, IT ROUNDED OFF A WONDERFUL EVENING FOR ME, AND IT CONVEYED A REAL SENSE OF OPTIMISM, MAKING ME LOOK FORWARD TO A FRESH START THE NEXT DAY. SOME COCKTAILS REALLY DO GIVE A "LIFT," AND I BELIEVE THIS COMBINATION OF GIN AND LUSCIOUS TOKAJI IS A FINE EXAMPLE.

Combine the ingredients in a shaker; fill up with ice. Stir gently for about 10 seconds. Strain into a glass filled with large chunks of ice (preferably triple-frozen—see page 157). Hold the lemon peel above the cocktail and gently twist to mist the surface, then rub the peel around the rim of the glass.

YOU CAN IMAGINE THE LOOK ON MY FACE WHEN A BIRDCAGE SPORTING A PAIR OF THE MOST BEAUTIFUL, PINK DELECTATIONS ARRIVED FOR ME AND MY HAPPY PARTNER ONE EVENING AT THE BEAUFORT BAR. CONCOCTED WITH ROMANCE IN MIND, THIS DRINK IS ALWAYS MADE IN PAIRS; HENCE THE INGREDIENTS GIVEN BELOW ARE ENOUGH FOR TWO. AS IN THE REST OF LIFE, THERE ARE SOME THINGS THAT CAN'T–OR SHOULDN'T–EXIST ON THEIR OWN.

THE GILDED CAGE

3oz. (70ml) strawberry Martini Rosato (see method)
10 strawberries
2oz. (50ml) fresh lemon juice
2oz. (50ml) Bombay Sapphire gin
1½oz. (40ml) sugar syrup
To garnish: strawberry foam (see page 159); freeze-dried raspberry powder

First, prepare the strawberry Martini Rosato and strawberry infusion. (If you don't have a pressure infuser, you can achieve a similar effect by chopping the strawberries and leaving them to infuse the Martini Rosato for 48 hours.) Combine the strawberry-infused Martini Rosato with the other ingredients in a shaker; fill up with ice. Shake; then double-strain into two Champagne flutes. Garnish with a layer of strawberry foam and the raspberry powder. To serve, place the glasses in a birdcage.

PROVENANCE

1 bar spoon (5ml) Bombay Sapphire gin
1½oz. (45ml) rhubarb poaching liquor
4oz. (125ml) rosé Champagne
To garnish: a tiny bowl of vanilla ice cream with a sprinkling of crisp (crumble) on top

CHRISTOPHER MAKES HIS OWN RHUBARB POACHING LIQUOR FOR THIS COCKTAIL, WHICH IS SERVED WITH A SMALL BOWL OF ICE CREAM AND CRUMBLE ON THE SIDE, THE IDEA BEING THAT THE ICE CREAM COATS THE MOUTH WHILE CONTRASTING WITH THE ACIDITY OF THE CHAMPAGNE AND THE SHARPNESS OF THE RHUBARB. AS I'M VERY INTERESTED IN FOOD AND DRINK PAIRING, I WAS KEEN TO TEST OUT THIS THEORY, AND I REALLY DO FIND THAT THE SWEET MORSELS ENHANCE THE COCKTAIL. THE UNFUSSY APPEARANCE OF THE DRINK BELIES THE COMPLEX TASTE.

Briefly stir all the ingredients over ice; strain into a Champagne flute. Serve with the tiny bowl of ice cream and crumble.

NO PRIZES FOR GUESSING THAT PIRATES ARE BEHIND THE NAMING OF THIS GREAT COCKTAIL, GIVEN THAT "THE PIRATES OF PENZANCE" WAS FIRST PERFORMED IN THE SAVOY THEATRE –OVER 130 YEARS AGO–AND THAT THE RECIPE USES RUM. WATCHING CHRISTOPHER AT WORK AT THE BAR, I WAS DELIGHTED TO SEE HIM INCLUDING IN THE MIX AN OLD FAVORITE OF MINE, GINGER BEER. THAT ADDITION SKILFULLY BRINGS TOGETHER THE DRINK'S DISPARATE INGREDIENTS.

PENZANCE

Combine the ingredients in a shaker; fill up with ice. Shake; then double-strain into a glass. Top up with ginger beer. Fill the glass with ice cubes and garnish with the mint, cherry, and pineapple.

1½oz. (40ml) Bacardi 8-year-old dark rum
2 bar spoons (10ml) peach liqueur
1oz. (25ml) fresh lemon juice
¾oz. (20ml) bird's eye chili-infused sugar syrup

4 fresh mint leaves
3 drops Angostura bitters
Ginger beer, to top up
To garnish: fresh mint sprig, marinated cherry, and compressed pineapple (vacuum packed)

CHRIS'S MOJITO

1oz. (30ml) fresh lime juice
¾oz. (20ml) sugar syrup
12 large fresh mint leaves
2oz. (60ml) Bacardi white rum
Soda water, to top up
To garnish: fresh mint sprig

HAVING DRUNK NUMEROUS MOJITOS IN AT LEAST A DOZEN DIFFERENT COUNTRIES–
I HAVE EVEN DRIVEN THROUGH THE STREETS OF NEW ORLEANS WITH MY FRIEND JULIA
CLASPING A MOJITO BETWEEN HER KNEES!–I REALIZE THAT CHRISTOPHER'S VERSION OF
THIS COCKTAIL IS AN ENTIRELY DIFFERENT ANIMAL, AND IT SERVES TO SHOW HIS TRUE
TALENTS. THE MUDDLED MINT, LIME JUICE, AND WHITE RUM ARE CLASSIC INGREDIENTS,
BUT CHRISTOPHER FAVORS SUGAR SYRUP RATHER THAN THE BROWN SUGAR THAT IS
OFTEN USED. THIS GIVES A VERY "CLEAN" RESULT AND MAKES THE DRINK LOOK FRESHER.

Combine the lime juice, sugar syrup, and mint leaves in a highball glass; add crushed ice to come about three-quarters of the way up. Churn vigorously with a bar spoon. Add the rum; churn again, making sure the mint is evenly distributed throughout. Top up with soda water and more crushed ice. Garnish with the mint sprig.

AMERICAN BAR
AT THE SAVOY

Top hat, white tie, and tails... these are what come to mind whenever I stroll into the American Bar at the Savoy, not only because the magnificently refurbished interior reminds me of the golden age of cocktails, when tails were de rigueur, but also because even details such as the cleverly shaped Champagne coolers lead one's thoughts in that direction. The room is mainly hewn from a black-and-white palette, with the largest black accent being the grand piano. Played nightly, it disgorges captivating tunes, often from when the American musical was—for me, at least—at its apogee, although I suspect the hotel's close connection with the adjoining Savoy Theatre is also a major influence. I am always delighted to see my bartender friend Erik Lorincz, who watches over things here. The cocktails cover the full gamut, from straight classics—of course—to carefully balanced interpretations of these iconic drinks as well as Erik's totally new creations. The American Bar at the Savoy, which must be one of the most famous cocktail bars in the world, is a great place to meet up with friends—after the theater, before lunch, whenever. I have also been known to pop in on my own, order a Smoky William Bloody Mary, and happily while away an hour just watching the scene around me.

1oz. (25ml) fresh lemon juice
1oz. (25ml) Cointreau
2oz. (50ml) Bombay Sapphire gin
½ white of 1 egg

WHITE LADY

SOME THINGS ARE BEST LEFT UNADORNED. THE WHITE LADY SEEN HERE IS UNDOUBTEDLY ONE, AS THE MARTINI GLASS IN WHICH IT IS SERVED IS SO GLAMOROUS THAT NO GARNISH IS NEEDED TO ATTRACT ATTENTION. BARTENDER ERIK THOROUGHLY CHILLED THE GLASS, WHICH WAS SPECIALLY MADE TO COMPLEMENT THE COCKTAIL, BEFORE POURING INTO IT HIS LIGHT, FROTHY, AND DELICIOUSLY CITRUSSY MIX.

Pre-chill the glass with ice. Pour all the ingredients into a shaker and fill with ice. Shake vigorously. Discard the ice in the glass. Strain the mixture into the glass.

IN SPRING 2011, I WAS ASKED, ALONG WITH TWO OR THREE FRIENDS, TO DECORATE A BANQUETING TABLE IN OUR VILLAGE TO CELEBRATE THE MARRIAGE OF PRINCE WILLIAM AND CATHERINE MIDDLETON. IT WAS AN EXCITING TIME NATIONWIDE, AND PEOPLE CAME UP WITH ALL KINDS OF TRIBUTES, INCLUDING THIS COCKTAIL INVENTED BY DANIEL BAERNREUTHER AT THE SAVOY. WHEN I DROPPED BY AT THE HOTEL'S AMERICAN BAR, IN THE WEEK BEFORE THE WEDDING, I COULDN'T RESIST TRYING IT. IT CAPTURED THE MOOD PERFECTLY.

ROYAL TRIBUTE

½ bar spoon (2.5ml) Green Chartreuse
½ bar spoon (2.5ml) maraschino liqueur
¾oz. (20ml) Martini Rosso vermouth
¾oz. (20ml) Bombay Sapphire gin
1 bar spoon (5ml) gomme syrup
Champagne, ice cold
To garnish: orange twist

Pre-chill a coupe glass. Pour all the ingredients, except the Champagne, over ice in a mixing jug. Stir. Strain into the glass. Top up with the Champagne and garnish with the orange twist.

KENTUCKY IS ONE OF THE PLACES I LOVE MOST IN THE STATES. THE
COUNTRYSIDE IS PARTICULARLY AGREEABLE, I HAVE FRIENDS THERE AND
I ENJOY GOING TO THE RACES WITH THEM. SO, WHEN I DISCOVERED THAT
RIP VAN WINKLE BOURBON IS MADE AT THE FAMILY DISTILLERY AT
LAWRENCEBURG IN KENTUCKY, I BECAME EVEN MORE HOOKED ON A VIEUX-
CARRÉ COCKTAIL. I'M TOLD IT ORIGINATES FROM THE LANDMARK
MONTELEONE HOTEL IN THE FRENCH QUARTER OF NEW ORLEANS.

VIEUX-CARRE

3 drops Angostura bitters
3 drops Peychaud's bitters
2 bar spoons (10ml)
Benedictine
1oz. (25ml) Rip Van
Winkle bourbon whiskey
1oz. (25ml) Antica
Formula vermouth
1oz. (25ml) Cognac
To garnish: orange twist

Pour all the ingredients over ice in a mixing jug.
Stir with a bar spoon. Remove the ice and put
in an old fashioned glass. Pour the cocktail into
the glass; add more ice if needed to top up.
Mist with the orange twist, then place it on
the cocktail.

MALACON

ONE OF MY EARLY MEMORIES OF ANYTHING TO DO WITH ALCOHOL WAS A VISIT TO A PORT LODGE IN
PORTUGAL, AND I WAS ASTOUNDED BY THE SCALE OF THE BUSINESS. AS I'M KEEN ON PORT–SO LONG
AS I DON'T HAVE TOO MUCH OF IT!–I SUSPECTED I WAS IN FOR A TREAT WHEN ERIK, WHO INVENTED
THIS COCKTAIL, ADDED SOME TO HIS SHAKER. HE DESCRIBES MALACON, WHICH IS NAMED AFTER
A PROMENADE IN CUBA, AS "BRIGHT, VIBRANT, AND A CELEBRATION OF LIFE." I WOULD AGREE.

1oz. (30ml) fresh lime
juice
2 bar spoons superfine
(caster) sugar
3 drops Peychaud's bitters
2oz. (50ml) Bacardi white
rum
2 bar spoons (10ml)
oloroso sherry
½oz. (15ml) ruby port

Pre-chill a glass with ice. Pour the
lime juice over ice in a shaker.
Add the rest of the ingredients.
Shake. Strain into the glass (having
discarded the ice used for chilling).
To serve, add a single lump of ice.

ABSINTHE DRIP

ABSINTHE'S REPUTATION FELL FROM GRACE WHEN IT WAS ASSOCIATED WITH LOW LIFE IN LOUCHE PARISIAN BARS AROUND THE TURN OF THE TWENTIETH CENTURY, BUT "THE GREEN FAIRY," AS THIS POTENT, BELLE EPOQUE DRINK WAS SOMETIMES CALLED, HAS BEEN REFORMULATED AND REHABILITATED IN RECENT YEARS. I'D EVEN GO SO FAR AS TO SAY THAT IT HAS BECOME RATHER CHIC—AND ABSINTHE DRIP, WITH ITS HAUNTINGLY BEAUTIFUL COLOR, DEFINITELY HAS A TOUCH OF THE FAIRYTALE ABOUT IT. THE SAVOY HAS A MAGNIFICENT CONTAINER FOR THE ICED WATER THAT IS DRIPPED ONTO THE SUGAR CUBE. JUST LOOK!

2oz. (50ml) absinthe
1 cube white sugar

Pour the absinthe into the glass. Place the sugar cube on a "drip," or straining, spoon positioned over the glass. Drip iced water slowly onto the cube so that the sugar dissolves through the strainer into the glass. Stir gently.

FERNET BRANCA IS SUPPOSED TO HAVE EXCELLENT DIGESTIVE QUALITIES AND I'VE MET MANY ITALIANS WHO SUBSCRIBE TO THIS HAPPY BELIEF. THE FACT THAT THE HANKY PANKY COCKTAIL WAS CREATED IN 1904 BY ADA COLEMAN, WHO WAS THE SAVOY'S FIRST-EVER FEMALE BARTENDER, GIVES IT ADDED CHARISMA. ERIK ALWAYS USES PUNT E MES VERMOUTH, WHICH HAS A DISTINCTIVE, BITTER-SWEET CHARACTER, AND "HARD" ICE BROKEN INTO CHUNKS (SEE PAGE 157). THIS KIND OF ICE IS ASTONISHINGLY CLEAR.

HANKY PANKY

1½ bar spoons (7.5ml) Fernet Branca

2oz. (50ml) Punt e Mes vermouth

2oz. (50ml) Bombay Sapphire gin

To garnish: orange twist

Pre-chill a glass. Stir all the ingredients over ice in a mixing jug (the cocktail should not be shaken, as this would "bruise" the gin); strain the mixture into the glass from high above, in order to aerate it. Mist the orange twist over the cocktail, then gently drop it into the glass

RAMOS FIZZ
(NEW ORLEANS FIZZ)

THIS DRINK WAS INVENTED ORIGINALLY IN THE 1880S BY ONE HENRY C. RAMOS AT HIS BAR IN NEW ORLEANS. THAT MUCH I HAVE DISCOVERED, BUT WHO WAS OLD TOM? HAVING TASTED GIN IN SOME OF THE MOST WONDERFUL BARS IN THE WORLD, I'M WELL AWARE THAT DIFFERENT BRANDS OF GIN PRODUCE VERY DIFFERENT RESULTS IN COCKTAILS, AND IT'S ALWAYS FUN TO TRY THE LESS OBVIOUS MAKES, SUCH AS OLD TOM. RAMOS FIZZ IS SERVED HERE IN A SHORT-STEMMED FLUTE IN THE SAME, BEAUTIFUL BLUE AS THE GLASS USED FOR THE WHITE LADY.

½oz. (15ml) fresh lemon juice
½oz. (15ml) fresh lime juice
3 bar spoons confectioner's (icing) sugar
3 drops orange flower water
2oz. (50ml) Old Tom gin
½ white of 1 egg
½oz. (15ml) heavy (double) cream
Soda water, to top up

Shake all the ingredients (except the soda water) over ice in a shaker. Strain into a cocktail glass with ice. Top up with the soda water.

CROQUET CLUB COBBLER

WHEN IT COMES TO MIXING THIS MORE COMPLEX VERSION OF A TRADITIONAL COBBLER, MY FEELING IS THAT
I WOULD PREFER TO PUT MY FAITH IN THE SAVOY AMERICAN BAR RATHER THAN TRUST MY LUCK AT THE LOCAL
CROQUET CLUB! BARTENDER ERIK, LIKE ALL COCKTAIL COGNOSCENTI, TENDS TO HAVE FAVORITE BRANDS OF
INGREDIENTS FOR HIS MIXES. FOR THIS LOVELY, FRUITY DRINK, HE PARTICULARLY RECOMMENDS THE ST GERMAIN
MAKE OF ELDERFLOWER LIQUEUR AND HENDRICK'S FOR THE GIN COMPONENT.

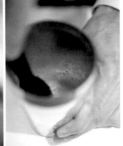

3 chunks fresh pineapple
(approx 1in./3cm cubes)
2 bar spoons superfine (caster)
sugar
Freshly squeezed juice of ½
lemon
2 bar spoons (10ml) fino sherry
½oz. (15ml) elderflower liqueur
1½oz. (45ml) Hendrick's gin
To garnish: 1 blueberry,
1 blackberry, 1 raspberry,
1 slice cucumber

Pre-chill a glass. Muddle the pineapple,
sugar, and lemon juice at the bottom of a
shaker. Add the rest of the ingredients and
top up with ice. Shake vigorously. Strain into
the chilled glass, with ice, and garnish with
the fruit and cucumber slice.

MOONWALK

IT'S JUST AS WELL THAT NEIL ARMSTRONG HADN'T BEEN
SAMPLING THIS COCKTAIL BEFORE BEING LET LOOSE IN HIS
ROCKET. IT PACKS QUITE A PUNCH! IT WAS CREATED IN 1969
BY THE THEN HEAD BARTENDER, JOE GILMORE, TO CELEBRATE
THE MOON-LANDING–NASA EVEN SENT THE SAVOY A "THANK-YOU"
LETTER FROM THE ASTRONAUT HIMSELF–AND IT HAS ATTRACTED
ADMIRERS EVER SINCE. THE WHITE SUGAR CUBE NOT ONLY
CAUSES THE COCKTAIL TO CHANGE AS YOU DRINK IT, BUT HAS
AN APPROPRIATELY LUNAR LOOK.

Stir all the ingredients (except the Champagne for topping up
and the sugar cube) over ice in a mixing jug or shaker. Put
the sugar cube into a Champagne flute and strain the mixture
over it. Top up with the Champagne. Mist the orange twist
over the top, then gently drop it into the cocktail.

5 drops orange flower water
5 drops grapefruit bitters
1oz. (30ml) Grand Marnier
¾oz. (20ml) Champagne
1 cube white sugar
Champagne (approximately
4oz./100ml), to top up
To garnish: orange twist

MY FRIEND TIM HAS A MARVELLOUS GLASS DECORATED WITH A COCKEREL. WHEN HE SHOWED IT TO ME, WE BOTH LAUGHED BECAUSE THE COCK HAS THE MOST WONDERFUL TAIL AND, NEEDLESS TO SAY, WE COULDN'T WAIT TO HAVE THE GLASS FILLED WITH–GUESS WHAT?–A COCKTAIL. ERIK OBLIGED WITH HIS GREEN PARK, WHICH HAS A SUPERB SILKINESS, THANKS TO THE EGG WHITE, BUT AN IMPORTANT PART OF CONFECTING THIS DELICACY IS THE DOUBLE-STRAINING. I ONLY WISH YOU COULD SEE THE COCKEREL MORE CLEARLY IN THE PICTURE!

6 leaves fresh basil
3 drops celery bitters
1oz. (25ml) fresh lemon juice
½oz. (15ml) sugar syrup
1½oz. (45ml) Old Tom gin
½ white of 1 egg
To garnish: fresh basil sprig

GREEN PARK

Fill a glass with crushed ice and set aside to chill. Put all the ingredients in a shaker and top up with ice. Shake. Discard the ice from the glass. Double-strain the mixture into the glass and garnish with the basil sprig.

THERE ARE TIMES IN LIFE, PARTICULARLY IN A HOT CLIMATE AND AFTER A LONG, HEAVY DAY, WHEN YOU YEARN TO HAVE A TALL, SOOTHING DRINK THAT'S ICE-COLD AND EXOTIC ENOUGH TO TRANSPORT YOU INTO A MORE RELAXED WORLD. DON'T THINK YOU HAVE TO BE AN OFFICER TO ENJOY THE SURPRISING MIX OF INGREDIENTS IN THIS COCKTAIL, WHICH INCLUDES AGAVE NECTAR AND VELVET FALERNUM, TOPPED OFF WITH A LIME TWIST AND CINNAMON STICK. AND DON'T THINK, EITHER, THAT THIS "NIGHTCAP" IS ONLY FOR LATE-NIGHT DRINKING!

OFFICER'S NIGHTCAP

First, fill a highball glass with ice and set aside. Add all the ingredients to a shaker. Give a quick stir and top up with ice. Shake. Strain any melted water from the glass but leave the ice in it. Strain the cocktail into the glass and garnish with the lime twist and cinnamon.

1oz. (25ml) fresh lime juice
2 bar spoons (10ml) Velvet Falernum
½oz. (15ml) agave nectar
½oz. (15ml) Ron Zacapa dark rum
2oz. (60ml) freshly pressed apple juice
2 bar spoons (10ml) Pimento Dram liqueur
To garnish: lime twist and cinnamon sticks

CARTE BLANCHE

ERIK TELLS ME HE HAD JAMES BOND IN MIND WHEN HE
MIXED THIS DRINK. I IMAGINE THAT WAS BECAUSE THE NAME
OF THE WHISKY–CROWN ROYAL–REMINDED HIM OF "CASINO
ROYALE," AND "CARTE BLANCHE" IS THE TITLE OF A JAMES
BOND NOVEL. WHATEVER THE THINKING, HE CAME UP WITH
A COMBINATION OF CANADIAN WHISKY AND COINTREAU THAT
I FOUND A REAL THRILLER. AS WITH MANY COCKTAILS, IT
IS ABSOLUTELY ESSENTIAL FOR THE GLASS TO BE WELL
CHILLED BEFOREHAND.

3 drops Angostura bitters
1oz. (30ml) Cointreau
2oz. (60ml) Crown Royal whisky

Chill a martini glass by filling it with ice. Put all
the ingredients into a mixing jug and top up
with ice. Stir. Discard the ice in the glass. Strain
the cocktail into the chilled glass. To serve, add
3 ice cubes from the mixing jug.

IT WOULD TAKE A LOT TO SEPARATE ME FROM MY JULEP, AS I FIND THE MEDLEY OF CRUSHED ICE, MINT, AND BOURBON AN IMMENSE TEMPTATION. ERIK GIVES THIS VERSION A SIGNATURE TWIST BY INTRODUCING CHERRY LIQUEUR AND THEN, RATHER FASCINATINGLY, TAKES IT TO ANOTHER LEVEL WITH A FEW DROPS OF CHOCOLATE BITTERS. TRADITIONALLY, A JULEP IS SERVED IN A SILVER BEAKER, A DRINKING VESSEL THAT NO SELF-RESPECTING BAR SHOULD BE WITHOUT.

JF JULEP

Handful fresh mint leaves (about 9)
2 bar spoons vanilla sugar
½oz. (15ml) Visciolata del Cardinale (Italian cherry liqueur)
½oz. (15ml) Woodford Reserve bourbon whiskey
5 drops The Bitter Truth Chocolate Bitters
To garnish: a black cherry and a fresh mint sprig

Stir all the ingredients together, with some crushed ice, in a silver beaker, gently muddling the mint. Top up with more crushed ice. Garnish with the cherry and mint.

I HAVE TO SAY I WAS FLATTERED WHEN ERIK CALLED THIS EXTRAORDINARY RENDITION OF A BLOODY MARY A SMOKY WILLIAM. THE COCKTAIL USES HIS VERY OWN "EL DIABLO" MIX (A SECRET RECIPE MADE, I GATHER, WITH FRESH CILANTRO, WORCESTERSHIRE SAUCE, SOY SAUCE, SHERRY, HORSERADISH, MUSTARD, CHILI PASTE, AND NAGA JOLOKIA CHILIES) AND IS SMOKED WITH HICKORY CHIPS, USING A SPECIAL "SMOKING GUN." WATCHING ERIK CARRY OUT THIS PROCESS MADE HIM SEEM MORE LIKE A SCIENTIST THAN A BARTENDER!

BLOODY MARY (SMOKY WILLIAM)

½oz. (15ml) "El Diablo" mix
2oz. (50ml) Ketel One vodka
2 bar spoons (10ml) freshly pressed tomato juice
To garnish: 3 tiny cocktail onions and a sprig of cilantro (coriander)

Combine all the ingredients in a shaker or mixing jug, then pour into a wine decanter with a broad base (a ship's decanter). Place some hickory wood chips into a "smoking gun" and blow the smoke into the decanter. Leave the drink just long enough for the aroma of the smoke to permeate it. Serve over ice in a highball glass and garnish with the onions and cilantro (coriander).

Freshly squeezed juice of ½ lime
3 drops The Bitter Truth Repeal Bitters
2 bar spoons (10ml) Pimento Dram liqueur
2oz. (50ml) Ron Zacapa dark rum
To garnish: lime twist; grated tonka bean

SWIZZLE

I CAN'T DENY THAT I HAVE BECOME A VERITABLE BARFLY OF LATE AND I AM ALWAYS INTRIGUED BY THE VARIETY OF TECHNIQUES AND EQUIPMENT I SEE BEING USED. FOR INSTANCE, I NOTICED THAT ERIK WIELDS A VERY PARTICULAR SORT OF SWIZZLE STICK WHEN BLENDING AND FROTHING THIS SWIZZLE COCKTAIL. BEING MADE OF WOOD ON THE CARIBBEAN ISLAND OF MARTINIQUE, THIS STICK IS INDISPUTABLY THE "REAL DEAL." A TWIST OF LIME AND A GRATING OF TONKA BEAN PUT THE FINAL TOUCH TO THIS MAGNIFICENT DRINK.

Combine all the ingredients in a tall glass. Fill three-quarters of the way up with crushed ice. Give a good swizzle with a swizzle stick. Top up with more crushed ice. Garnish with a lime twist and a few gratings of tonka beans.

THE KNOWLEDGE

I am the first to admit that I adore going to cocktail bars—the best cocktail bars, that is!—but that doesn't mean to say I don't revel in making cocktails at home. In fact, it was probably thanks to having visited some of the world's greatest bars that I became inspired to try my hand at cocktails myself. Now, not only do I regularly make cocktails at home for my own pleasure but I also find that these shaken and stirred mixes are brilliant for when I have guests. They are the perfect party drinks, as they provide good conversation openers, especially for guests who may not have met before. In the following pages are recipes for my top-ten favorite cocktails, plus recipes for the canapés I serve with them at parties. I have a great little team to help me with my parties: Alastair, the mixologist; Kate, the canapé-maker; and Daniel the butler. Given my interest in crystal—and in glassware as a whole—it is not surprising that I take special care with this aspect of serving cocktails. You will find here a selection of designs that I would recommend for the drinks featured in this book, plus some useful tips for cocktails in general.

WILLIAM'S PARTY DRINKS

THERE ARE PROBABLY ABOUT 30 COCKTAILS THAT I ESPECIALLY LOVE AND SERVE AT HOME, BUT FOR THESE PAGES I SET MYSELF THE CHALLENGE OF WHITTLING THEM DOWN TO TEN. WHAT A STRUGGLE TO BE SO DISCIPLINED!

I chose my "top ten" cocktails with one important factor in mind: they are all relatively simple to make. Even flaming the orange zest for the Cosmopolitan isn't that difficult (and it does impart the most wonderful flavor). Some of the recipes for my favorite cocktails are variations on others in this book, but, as we all know, even a seemingly small difference in the ingredients and quantities can alter the outcome considerably. However, in a couple of cases, the recipes are sufficiently similar that I have simply cross-referred to the chapters where you can find "the mixes."

If I have invited round only a few friends, I enjoy making the drinks myself, but for a larger party I enlist the help of Alastair, a professional mixologist. He and I discuss the possibilities beforehand and come up with a short selection, based on my favorites, which would be appropriate for the occasion.

The selection depends to some extent on the time of day and the time of year. At midday, for instance, I may well offer a Bloody Mary, but I wouldn't do that in the evening. In winter, I always ensure there is something "warming," whereas in summer my starting point would probably be a long, cool concoction, such as a mojito.

I also vary the cocktails according to whether the party is in my apartment in London, where the atmosphere is more sophisticated, or in my house in the country where, if the weather is balmy, I like to lure everyone out into the garden. Chatting with friends on a sunny day in Gloucestershire, with the heavenly scent of roses in the air and an exquisitely colored Cosmopolitan in my hand, is my idea of bliss.

MARGARITA

Freshly squeezed juice of 1 lime
2½ bar spoons (12.5ml) agave syrup
1¼oz. (35ml) tequila
½oz. (15ml) triple sec
To garnish: lime twist

Prepare the glass with a salt (or sugar) rim. Put the ingredients in a shaker, with ice, and shake. Strain into the glass and garnish with the lime twist.

RUSTY NAIL

1oz. (25ml) Drambuie
1oz. (25ml) Scotch whisky
To garnish: lemon twist

Run the lemon twist gently round the rim of the glass, then place in glass. Pour in the Drambuie and whisky; add ice. Stir 10 times with a bar spoon—this is enough to infuse the lemon without diluting the cocktail too much with the ice. Top up with more ice cubes. (Putting a lot of ice in the glass will keep the temperature of the cocktail very cold, so the ice will melt slowly and the cocktail will develop as you drink it.)

COSMOPOLITAN WITH FLAMING ORANGE ZEST

Freshly squeezed juice of ½ lime
1¼oz. (35ml) vodka
½oz. (15ml) triple sec
½oz. (15ml) cranberry juice
To garnish: 3 raspberries; orange zest, flamed

First, fill the glass with ice and set aside to chill. Put all the ingredients in a shaker, with ice, and shake vigorously. Discard the ice from the glass, strain the cocktail into the glass —it will be a delicate shade of pink —and garnish with the raspberries skewered on a cocktail pick. For the orange garnish, hold the strip of zest by one end; gently (and carefully!) bring a lighter up to it to release the oils; then hold the zest above the cocktail and twist it to "mist" the oils over the top of the drink. Finally, run the flamed zest round the rim of the glass. Discard the zest.

CLASSIC GIN MARTINI

1 bar spoon (5ml) dry vermouth
3oz. (75ml) gin
To garnish: 2 or 3 olives

This cocktail needs to be served
very cold, so make sure the glass is
well chilled beforehand; you could
chill the bottles of vermouth and
gin in the freezer. Fill the shaker
or mixing jug with ice, pour the
vermouth over the ice and stir a
few times with a bar spoon. Add
the gin, stir 10 times—no more,
as the cocktail could become too
diluted with water from the ice.
Strain the cocktail into the chilled
glass and garnish with the olives
skewered on a cocktail pick.

LONG WATERMELON MARTINI

7 chunks watermelon, about 1in. (2–3cm)
Freshly squeezed juice of I lemon
2oz. (50ml) vodka
2½ bar spoons (12.5ml) sugar syrup
To garnish: small wedge watermelon

Put the watermelon chunks and
lemon juice in a shaker and muddle
until smooth; then add the vodka
and sugar syrup, plus ice. Shake.
Double-strain into a glass with
plenty of crushed ice. For the
garnish, insert a straw through
the watermelon wedge, carefully
remove the straw, and squeeze out
the watermelon pulp; then re-insert
the straw into the hole in the
wedge. Place the wedge on the
rim of the glass, with the straw
in the cocktail.

MERRY ROSE

Lime wedge
Sugar
2¼oz. (60ml) vodka
2 bar spoons (10ml) grenadine
3oz. (75ml) pink grapefruit juice
1 bar spoon (5ml) fresh lime juice
2 bar spoons (10ml) Cointreau
1 bar spoon (5ml) cherry brandy (optional)
To garnish: candied (glacé) cherry

Prepare the glass with a sugar rim:
run the cut side of the lime wedge
round the rim; then dip the rim in
sugar. Pour the vodka, grenadine,
grapefruit and lime juice, and
Cointreau into a shaker, with ice.
Shake. Strain into the prepared
glass, add plenty of crushed ice. If
wished, drizzle the cherry brandy
over the top. Garnish with a candied
cherry speared on a cocktail pick.

GIN SLING

Freshly squeezed juice of ½ lemon
2½ barspoons (12.5ml) sugar syrup
1½oz. (35ml) gin
½oz. (15ml) cherry brandy
Soda water, to top up

Put all the ingredients, except the soda water, into
a shaker, with ice. Shake vigorously and strain
into a pre-chilled glass. Top up with soda water.

WHISKEY SOUR

1 egg
Freshly squeezed juice of 1 lemon
2½ bar spoons (12.5ml) sugar syrup
2oz. (50ml) bourbon whiskey
A few drops Angostura Bitters (optional)
To garnish: lemon zest

Hold the cocktail strainer over the shaker and use it to catch
the yolk, which should be discarded. Ease the spring off the
strainer and place it in the shaker with the egg white (this will
whisk the white more effectively while the cocktail is being
shaken). Add the remaining ingredients to the shaker and
shake vigorously. Pour into a rocks glass filled with ice cubes.
Garnish with the lemon zest.

NEGRONI

This is one of my favorite cocktails where the
recipe I follow overlaps with one given by
a bartender in this book: turn to page 36 in
The Connaught Bar chapter to see it.

MOJITO

It's probably better not to attempt to count the number of
mojitos I have drunk during my travels—and at home! The
recipe I favor at home is pretty well the same as bartender
Christopher's at the Beaufort Bar at the Savoy, which you
can find on page 110

WILLIAM'S PARTY GLASSES

ILLUSTRATED HERE ARE SOME OF MY FAVORITE
GLASSES FOR SERVING COCKTAILS IN MY
HOME. BENEATH THE NAMES OF THE DESIGNS
I HAVE SUGGESTED WHICH OF THE EXQUISITE
DRINKS GARNERED IN THIS BOOK WOULD BE
APPROPRIATE IN THESE GLASSES.

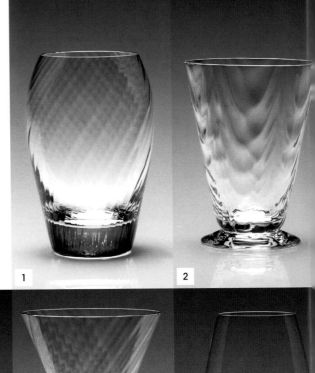

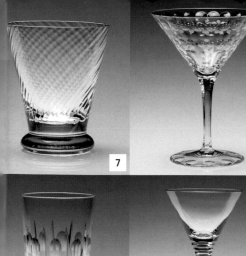

1 ATLANTIC SPIRAL GLASS

Shogun Old-Fashioned
Tea Rinfresco
Yellow Submarine
The Sorcerer

2 ROXIE DOF

Negroni
Gin Lane
New Dawn
Bloody Mary

3 LALLY CHAMPAGNE FLUTE

Vintage Champagne
Elixir

4 VESTA CHAMPAGNE FLUTE

Peach and Cardamom Bellini
Al Fresco Bellini

5 CALYPSO WINE GLASS

Green Lady
Almond Espresso Martini
Green Park
Absinthe Drip

6 LONDON WHITE WINE

Celebration Cup
The Gilded Cage
Croquet Club Cobbler
Cosmopolitan

7 SPIRAL-FOOTED TUMBLER

Vieux Carré
Old-Fashioned
JF Julip
Whiskey Sour

8 ERNESTINE MARTINI GLASS

Connaught Martini
Annabel's Classic Martini
White Lady
Merry Rose

9 CORRINE OLD-FASHIONED TUMBLER

Bloody Mary
Horse's Neck
Rusty Nail

10 CORRINE TALL COCKTAIL TUMBLER

Sun Crushed
Swizzle
Kentucky
Penzance
Gin Sling

11 KELLY HIBALL TUMBLER

Raspberry and Rose Mojito
Mojito
Officer's Nightcap
Croquet Club Cobbler

12 VESTA MARTINI GLASS

Tricolore
Caramel Rob Roy
Amber Manhattan

13 KELLY MARTINI GLASS

Dry Martini
Ramos Fizz
Margarita
Classic Gin Martini

14 LILLIAN TALL MARTINI GLASS

Ristretto Manhattan
Dragon
Apple Martini

WILLIAM'S PARTY CANAPES

CHEESE STRAWS

Makes about 40; best eaten slightly warm

1 sheet ready-rolled puff pastry
1 egg, beaten
1 cup (150g) strong Cheddar cheese, grated
Paprika

Brush the pastry with beaten egg; sprinkle with half the cheese and a pinch of paprika. Press the cheese into the pastry, then carefully turn the pastry over. Brush with egg, sprinkle with the remaining cheese and another pinch of paprika, then press the cheese in.

Preheat the oven to 350°F/180°C/gas 4. Cut ½-in. (1-cm) wide strips across the shorter length of the pastry; twist the strips into spirals and place on a parchment-lined baking sheet, 2in. (5cm) apart. Bake for about 10 minutes, until golden. Cool on a wire rack.

PARMESAN AND CHILI SHORTBREADS WITH CHÈVRE, ROASTED TOMATO, AND PESTO

Makes about 40

FOR THE SHORTBREAD
1¼ cups (120g) all-purpose (plain) flour, sifted
½ cup (120g) Parmesan cheese, grated
7 tablespoons (100g) cold butter, diced
Large pinch chili flakes
Pinch salt

FOR THE TOMATOES
20 cherry tomatoes
Salt
Pinch sugar
Olive oil

TO FINISH
¾ cup (200g) chèvre cheese, crumbled
⅓ cup (100g) pesto
40 fried basil leaves (optional)

Put the shortbread ingredients in a food processor and pulse to form a smooth dough. Roll out to a thickness of ¼in. (5mm) and stamp out rounds with a 1½in. (4cm) pastry cutter. Place rounds on parchment-lined baking sheets and chill for 30 minutes. Preheat the oven to 350°F/180°C/gas 4, and bake until golden, about 8–10 minutes. Cool on a wire rack.

Preheat the oven to 400°F/200°C/gas 6. Cut the cherry tomatoes in half, place cut-side up on a parchment-lined baking sheet, sprinkle with salt and sugar, and drizzle with oil. Place in the preheated oven, then immediately reduce temperature to 250°F/120°C/gas ½. Let the tomatoes roast for a couple of hours.

To finish, top each shortbread with some crumbled chèvre, a roasted tomato-half, and a tiny dollop of pesto. Decorate with a fried basil leaf, if liked.

FILO TARTLETS WITH SMOKED SALMON AND SOUR CREAM

Makes about 24

FOR THE TARTLETS
Butter, for greasing
A few sheets phyllo (filo) pastry
Melted butter, for brushing

FOR THE FILLING
8oz. (250g) smoked salmon, sliced
½ cup (120g) sour cream or crème fraîche
Freshly ground black pepper
Bunch fresh chives, snipped

Preheat the oven to 325°F/170°C/gas 3. Butter 2 12-hole, mini-muffin pans. Cut the pastry into 2-in. (5-cm) squares. Take 3 squares and make a star shape by layering them at slightly different angles, brushing with melted butter between each layer. Press a star shape into each muffin hole. Bake until golden, about 8 minutes. Remove from pans and cool on a wire rack.

Fill each tartlet with some sliced smoked salmon and a teaspoon of sour cream; add a grinding of black pepper and some snipped chives.

SPICED SALMON FISHCAKES WITH MANGO AND LIME SALSA

Makes 25–30

FOR THE FISHCAKES
10oz. (300g) salmon fillet, lightly poached in salted water
10oz. (300g) Desirée potatoes, boiled in salted water and mashed
1 fresh red chili, finely chopped
1 tablespoon tomato ketchup
2 tablespoons mayonnaise
3 tablespoons chopped fresh cilantro (coriander)
Salt and freshly ground black pepper
Fresh breadcrumbs
Oil, for greasing

FOR THE SALSA
1 shallot, finely diced
1 lime, peeled, segmented (no pith) and finely chopped
1 ripe mango, peeled and finely diced
1 teaspoon chopped fresh mint
Small pinch salt

TO FINISH
Sour cream (crème fraîche)

For the fishcakes, flake the salmon and mix together with the remaining ingredients (except breadcrumbs and oil). Chill for a few hours, then form the mixture into patties about 1¼in. (3cm) diameter. Preheat the oven to 350°F/180°C/gas 4. Coat with breadcrumbs and bake on lightly-oiled, parchment-lined baking sheets for about 20 minutes.

For the salsa, gently mix together all the ingredients. To finish, top each fishcake with a tiny blob of sour cream, followed by a teaspoon of the salsa.

FIGS WITH GORGONZOLA AND PROSCIUTTO

Cut ripe figs into quarters, and cut each slice of ham into 3 or 4 long strips. Take a small piece of Gorgonzola cheese, place on a fig segment, and wrap a slice of ham around to secure.

GAZPACHO WITH FRESH CRAB

Enough for about 35 shot glasses

4 slices white bread, crusts removed
1 tablespoon red wine vinegar
1 garlic clove, chopped
1 tablespoon superfine (caster) sugar
⅓ cup (75ml) olive oil
1½lb (700g) ripe plum tomatoes, chopped
2 cups (500ml) tomato juice
6 scallions (spring onions), chopped
1 cucumber, chopped
2 red bell peppers, chopped
A handful fresh basil leaves
Salt and freshly ground black pepper

TO FINISH
8oz. (250g) fresh crab (white meat only)
Basil oil, or olive oil, for drizzling

In a food processor, blend together the bread, vinegar, garlic, and sugar, then add the remaining ingredients and process to a smooth purée. Season to taste with salt and pepper and pass through a strainer (sieve) for a finer texture. Chill for at least 4 hours. Serve in shot glasses, topped with half a teaspoon crab meat and a drizzle of oil.

CRISPY WONTON WRAPPERS WITH SHRIMP, AVOCADO, AND WASABI

Makes about 25 wrappers

Wonton wrappers
Vegetable oil, for frying
1 ripe avocado, peeled and chopped
1 tablespoon mayonnaise
½ teaspoon wasabi paste
A squeeze fresh lime juice
25 large, cooked, peeled shrimp (prawns)

TO FINISH
Pickled ginger
Pea shoots (optional)

Cut the wonton wrappers into quarters and deep-fry, 3 or 4 at a time, in a small pan, filled one-third full with vegetable oil. The wrappers will take just a few seconds in the hot oil to become crisp and golden. Remove the crisps with a slotted spoon and drain on absorbent paper towels.

Mix the avocado with the mayonnaise, wasabi, and lime juice.

To assemble, top each wonton crisp with a teaspoon of avocado mixture; add a shrimp, a sliver of pickled ginger, and a pea shoot, if using.

RASPBERRY AND PISTACHIO PAVLOVAS

Makes about 25

2 egg whites, at room temperature
½ cup (125g) superfine (caster) sugar

FOR FILLING
1¼ cups (300ml) heavy (double) cream, whipped
⅓ cup (50g) pistachios, shelled and chopped
About 25 raspberries
Confectioner's (icing) sugar

Preheat oven to 250°F/120°C/gas ½. Whisk the egg whites until soft-peak stage, then add the sugar, a tablespoon at a time, whisking well after each addition, until the mixture is stiff and glossy.

Using a small, plain nozzle, pipe ¾in. (2cm) diameter discs of the mixture onto parchment-lined baking sheets, building up the outside edge of the discs by piping a second layer round the perimeter. Space the discs 1in. (2.5cm) apart.

Bake until firm to the touch, about 40 minutes. Remove from the parchment when cool; fill with whipped cream and sprinkle with chopped pistachios. Top with a raspberry and dust with sifted confectioner's sugar.

TIPS, TERMS, AND TECHNIQUES

CHILLING GLASSES Many cocktails in this book call for a well-chilled glass. One safe way to do this is to fill the appropriate glass with ice and leave until it feels very cold to the touch. Discard the ice before pouring the cocktail into the glass.

DASHES AND DROPS It is quite difficult to be precise about these measures. However, a dash is generally thought of as a slightly larger quantity than a drop and is approximately equivalent to ¼ teaspoon (1–2ml). For a drop, think of the amount of liquid you would get if using a dropper. However, as these measurements are used for strongly flavored liquids, the amount you use depends to a large extent on personal taste.

BAR SPOON A long-handled, metal spoon, sometimes with a bowl at each end, used for stirring and muddling. The bowl usually holds 5ml, which can be useful for measuring.

CELERY AIR Agostino Perrone's Bloody Mary (page 17) is crowned with this, which he makes by juicing celery with a small amount of celery salt and Lecite. Most "airs" can be made similarly by blending vegetable or fruit juice with Lecite in a large bowl and skimming off the "air" from the top. You could use a stick blender for blending.

FLAMING To do this, a piece of citrus peel is held at one end and a lighter brought up to it in order to release some of the oils. The peel is then held over the glass and twisted, to create a fine mist that falls onto the top of the cocktail (see Twist.) The flaming produces a particularly aromatic mist.

GLASSES Although specific shapes are used for classic cocktails, such as martinis, you can be more adventurous if serving "newer" or exotic concoctions. Ideally, you should have in your cupboard the following traditional shapes: martini, highball, old fashioned, Champagne flute, coupe, and goblet. For juleps, a silver beaker is ideal. And, of course, wine glasses can often be appropriate. You can find some suggestions for glasses on pages 150–151.

ICE Many bartenders use "hard" ice, which is diamond-clear. Apart from looking wonderful, it takes longer to melt than ordinary ice, so the rate at which it dilutes the cocktail is slower and the drink remains at the perfect temperature for longer. Machine-made "hard" ice, which is double- or triple-frozen, is usually produced in large chunks, which the bartender "chisels" into smaller pieces (though still quite big, as he wants to keep the cocktail as cold as possible).

You can make this kind of ice at home by freezing an ice-cube tray of water in the normal way. Once frozen, remove it from the freezer and allow to thaw. (This forces out the tiny oxygen bubbles that cause ice to look cloudy and it will make the final ice more compact—hence the name "hard.") Then re-freeze the thawed ice. Repeat the process for triple-frozen ice. Although "hard"

ice is the ultimate for cocktail-making, ordinary ice is generally acceptable for the "home" bar.

If a recipe calls for crushed ice, and you don't have a machine for making this, the simplest way to achieve it is to put ice cubes in a single layer between two clean dish towels, on a flat, sturdy surface, and bash with a wooden rolling pin.

INFUSING When a recipe includes an ingredient "infused" with a particular flavor, you can often buy the product ready-made. However, in some instances, you may have to do the infusing yourself. Generally, this is a simple matter of steeping the flavoring—strawberries, for instance—in the liquid, possibly sugar syrup, long enough for it to impart its flavor.

Some infusions are rather more complicated, such as in the Walnut and Maple Old-Fashioned (page 82), which uses walnut-infused whiskey. Bartender Adam Jannese lightly toasts roughly-chopped walnuts and adds them to the Eagle bourbon, which he then heats in a baby-bottle warmer for sufficient time to infuse the whiskey with the flavor of the nuts.

The Patience cocktail (page 88) uses sugar syrup infused with green tea and cucumber. At the Beaufort Bar, this is made as follows: prepare a sugar syrup with 2 parts sugar and 1 part water, then add 2 teaspoons (10ml) loose-leaf green tea per 33fl. oz. (1 litre) of syrup, stir and leave to steep for 3 minutes; strain. Put 1 whole cucumber, cut into strips, in a sealable container and add the syrup; stir, allow to steep overnight, then strain.

MEASUREMENTS The quantities in this book are in US and metric measurements. Do not mix the two. For simplicity, you can calculate 25ml or 30ml to 1oz. This is not precise but is usually fine for preparing cocktails. The important thing to remember with any recipe is to stick to either 25ml or 30ml to 1oz, as the type of measurement used is less critical than the ratio between the ingredients. If a cocktail is made up of 1oz. (30ml) Cointreau and 2oz. (60ml) whisky, this could be represented as 1 part Cointreau and 2 parts whisky. So long as that ratio is retained, it does not matter if you use millilitres or fluid ounces. The following conversions are approximate:
1fl. oz. = 25–30ml
1 bar spoon/teaspoon = 5ml
1 tablespoon = 15ml

A useful device for measuring is a metal "jigger" (see below), which is in fact two "thimbles," joined together, each holding a specific amount.

SHAKERS There are two main types of shakers. The most convenient one is made up of three parts: a tall beaker, a pierced lid that can act as a strainer, and a cap that covers the strainer. After the cocktail is shaken, the cap is removed and the drink poured through the lid/strainer into the glass. If the cocktail does not need to be strained, both the cap and the lid/strainer are removed. The other type of shaker is usually referred to as a "Boston shaker." This has only two parts, both shaped like beakers, which fit together for shaking. One part is usually made of glass and the other of metal. There is no "built-in" strainer in the Boston shaker.

MIST AND MISTING See Twist

MIXING Some cocktails are "mixed" rather than shaken. The simplest vessel to use for mixing is a jug, as it has a pouring lip, but you could also use a shaker without the lid. The mixing of the cocktail is done by stirring the ingredients together, with or without ice, before being poured into a glass. Some cocktails are mixed directly in the glass in which they are served.

MUDDLING This involves putting solid ingredients, such as slices of fruit and mint leaves, in a mixing jug or shaker, either on their own or with other ingredients, and then pressing/crushing them with the back of a bar spoon or a "muddler" (a pestle). The idea is to release the fruit juices and the leaf flavors.

RHUBARB POACHING LIQUOR This is one of the ingredients in the Provenance cocktail (page 106). Bartender Christopher Moore combines 2 parts Champagne with

1 part vanilla syrup and 1 part sugar syrup. He uses 2 sticks of rhubarb (cleaned and chipped) per 33fl. oz. (1 litre) of poaching liquid, then vacuum-packs it on medium before placing it in a water bath set to 140°F/60°C for 24 hours. Then he strains it and allows to cool completely before using. You could approximate this recipe by gently poaching the rhubarb in the liquid in a saucepan for about 20 minutes before straining and cooling.

SALT AND SUGAR RIMS Some cocktails benefit from being drunk from a glass with the rim covered with a layer of salt or sugar (or, sometimes, with something more exotic, such as cocoa powder). First rub the rim of the glass with the cut side of a wedge of citrus fruit or with zest to create a sticky surface. (If you hold the glass upside-down, there is less chance of the juice running down the sides of the glass or into it.) Then dip the rim in salt or sugar. Shake off excess salt or sugar; none must fall into the glass.

SQUEEZING CITRUS FRUIT If the fruit feels hard, "massage" it in your hands before squeezing it, as this helps to extract the juice. Some bartenders, including Agostino Perrone of the Connaught Bar, often use a "Mexican elbow" squeezer (see above). This type

of squeezer has two "cups," one of which is pierced to allow the juice to run out when the second "cup" is clamped down into it. Thin-skinned citrus fruits tend to be better for juicing.

STRAINING AND DOUBLE-STRAINING

Many cocktails have to be strained to ensure that solid ingredients and ice are not transferred from the shaker or mixing jug to the glass. If the cocktail only needs to be strained once, then a shaker with a built-in strainer will do the job.

If it needs to be double-strained, you must have a second, separate strainer. Double-straining is often necessary in cocktails, such as martinis, where the ingredients are shaken over ice but it is important to avoid even small shards of ice falling into the glass. The cocktail is poured through the strainer in the lid of the shaker, while a second, fine strainer is held over the glass. The spring-loaded type of strainer is also useful, especially if you have to strain a cocktail made in a Boston shaker or mixing jug.

STRAWBERRY FOAM Some cocktails have a layer of "foam" on top, giving a luxurious froth through which the liquid is drunk. Bartender Christopher Moore makes the strawberry-flavored foam in the recipe for Gilded Cage (page 105) with 3 punnets strawberries, ¾ cup (200ml) water, ⅓ cup (100ml) sugar syrup, ⅔ cup (150ml) egg white, 3g Lecite. He blends the strawberries with the water and sugar syrup, then fine-strains the mixture, blends again with the egg white and the Lecite sprinkled on top. He transfers this to a cream-whipper and gases twice.

These quantities make a large amount of foam and Christopher uses a cream-whipper, but you could scale-down the ingredients and you could try to get the same effect by using a hand-held frother (the sort for making cappuccinos) or electric whisk.

SUGAR SYRUP This syrup, which is sometimes called "Simple syrup," is used as a sweetener in many cocktails as it gives a clearer appearance and cleaner taste than adding undissolved sugar straight into the drink. You can buy this readymade or make your own. A general-purpose syrup can be prepared with 1½ measures super-fine (caster) sugar to 1 measure water. Put both ingredients in a saucepan and heat, stirring, until the sugar is completely dissolved. (If the solution reaches boiling point, do not allow it to boil for long or it will become too thick.) Allow to cool completely before storing in a bottle in the fridge. It should keep for 2–3 months.

Some cocktail recipes stipulate a slightly thicker syrup, in which case use 2 parts sugar to one part water, or a lighter one made with equal parts sugar and water.

Sugar syrups can be infused with a flavoring, such as tea or cucumber. See Infusing.

TWIST This usually refers to a strip of citrus peel, about 2in. (5cm) long. For misting, it is held over the drink and twisted, so that the oils in the peel are released in a fine mist that falls onto the surface of the drink. (Use a potato peeler to remove the peel from the fruit, being careful not to include any of the bitter white pith. It is easier if you use fruit with thick skins.)

INDEX

TO ENJOY A COCKTAIL

ANNABEL'S
Members only club
46 Berkeley Square, Mayfair
London W1J 5AT
+44 207 629 1096
www.annabels.co.uk

THE AMERICAN BAR
THE BEAUFORT BAR
The Savoy Hotel
Strand
London WC2R 0EU
+ 44 207 836 4343
www.fairmont.com/savoy

THE CONNAUGHT BAR
The Connaught
Carlos Place
London W1K 2AL
+ 44 207 499 7070
www.the-connaught.co.uk

THE BLUE BAR
The Berkeley
Wilton Place
London SW1X 7RL
+ 44 207 235 6000
www.the-berkeley.co.uk

WEBSITES AND ADDRESSES

To find out more about the crystal used in this book and
for a global stockists list including the USA, please visit
www.williamyeowardcrystal.com

To view the collections in the United Kingdom, including
crystal, furniture, fabrics, and accessories, please visit

WILLIAM YEOWARD
270 Kings Road London SW3 5AW
+ 44 207 349 7828
store@williamyeoward.com
www.williamyeoward.com